A PATH OF
BEAUTY

An Artist's Devotional

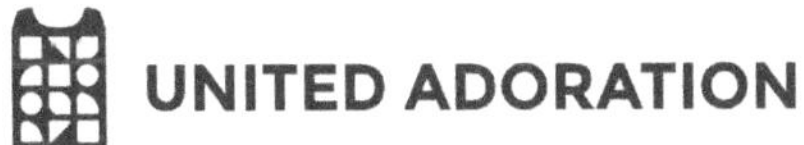
UNITED ADORATION

United Adoration
921 E. Dupont Rd., Suite 893
Fort Wayne, IN 46825
www.unitedadoration.com / www.unitedadoration.org.uk

978-1-7379278-2-2 (paperback)
978-1-7379278-3-9 (ebook)

Contents

A Note From The Editors ii

Foreword: A Path of Beauty iii

Introduction: How to Use this Book viii

PART ONE: Walking with our Creator 1

    1. The Secret Place 2

    2. Reclaiming Childlike Wonder 6

    3. Creating From Covenant 10

    4. Trinity, Creation, and the Artist 14

    5. Stones of Remembrance 19

    Reflective & Artistic Practices 23

PART TWO: Walking with our Calling 27

    6. What is an Artist? 28

    7. What is Beauty? 32

    8. A Beautiful Waste 37

    9. Remade in the Making 41

    10. The Artist's Conscience 45

    Reflective & Artistic Practices 49

PART THREE: Walking with our Craft 53

    11. Sowing and Sabbath 54

    12. Birthing Universes 58

    13. Diligence as an Offering 62

    14. The Slipstream of Stewardship 66

    15. You Are Loosed! 70

    Reflective & Artistic Practices 74

PART FOUR: Walking with the Kingdom 77

16. The Thin Places of Our Lives 78

17. Imago Dei 83

18. A Heart of Humility 88

19. In Unwanted Places 92

20. Multiplying Light 96

Reflective & Artistic Practices 100

PART FIVE: Walking Forward 103

21. Make That Art 104

Concluding Reflective Practice 107

Contributor Biographies 110

Acknowledgements 116

A Note From The Editors

From its inception, we wanted this devotional to be representative of the global organisation that United Adoration has become. To that end, we are delighted to have contributors representing the SE Asian, British, and American branches of UA. This did, however, present us with an editorial dilemma: American English or British English?! We have chosen to retain the variant used by each contributor, so you will find both American and British spellings used from chapter to chapter. We trust this adds colour, and not confusion, to the reading experience!

A Path of Beauty

BY REV. DAVE FRINCKE

Bleak. Brown. Lifeless. Mile after mile I stared out the window as we drove through the wilderness of Egypt. I had driven through deserts before, but this felt different. Maybe because not driving allowed me to fix my full attention on the landscape. Or, most probably, it was because my wife Bethany and I were on a spiritual pilgrimage and my soul was particularly tender towards God.

We were on the journey of a lifetime called "The Exodus Tour" which followed the path of the Israelites beginning in Egypt, through Jordan, and into Israel. It was my first time in this part of the world and I was soaking it all in.

Let me pause to say that there is something you need to know about me. I have a very active imagination. Actually, maybe a more accurate way to describe it is, a "crazy weird holy imagination." But let's go with Holy Imagination for short. Though I don't build theology from it, I have found Holy Imagination to be a wonderful tool to help me engage with the Scriptures in a deep way.

As the long drive continued, I kept thinking, "This is the actual place where the Israelites walked, discovered the character of God, and built His Tabernacle." My Holy Imagination kicked into high gear. *What did it look like for the Israelites to assemble, disassemble, and carry this structure called the Tabernacle? When it was set up and the people encamped all around, what did the formation look like from a distance? How long did it take to walk from the edge of the camp to the Outer Courts?*

THE TABERNACLE

God gave Moses a lot of details regarding the construction of the Tabernacle. A LOT of details. It probably seemed overwhelming to Moses, Bezalel, and all the artists involved in its creation. But those details mattered to God; they weren't frivolous to Him. He specifically instructed that the curtains of the Tabernacle were to include fine twined linen and blue, purple, and scarlet yarns. The veil too was to have the same colors included. Worked into all of this were to be wonderful works of art—skillful depictions of Cherubim. But have you ever asked yourself what including the colors and the Cherubim actually accomplished? What did they add to the function of the Tabernacle? Did they make the sacrifices better?

Those questions seem silly. But those are the kinds of questions many modern church-goers often ask about spending precious resource on the arts. The truth is, God's instructions to include colors and artwork into the Tabernacle didn't make it functionally better or more efficient. The colors and artwork helped make the Tabernacle beautiful.

BEAUTY IN THE DESERT

Looking out into the endless sea of bleakness and blandness, I imagined millions of people surrounding this other-worldly structure called the Tabernacle. I imagined the journey of walking from the outskirts of the camp towards the very Presence of God for the first time. And I imagined peering into the curtained area—seeing the colors and the artwork standing out in stark contrast against the brown, lifeless desert. Maybe this really was heaven on earth. What a journey. What a sight to see. I imagined myself, a person just getting to know who God is, realizing in that moment that He wanted me to know something—beauty was important to Him.

God has hard-wired humans to appreciate beauty. We are mesmerized by it. We are drawn to it. It feeds our soul. In its purest form, this is a gift from God to humanity. God knows this. His purposeful inclusion of beauty in the Tabernacle was not insignificant. He was showing us how much He cares about beauty and the human desire for it. In the midst of a brown and lifeless desert, He wanted His people to find the beauty their souls longed for in His Presence. A path towards God is a path towards beauty.

Our "Exodus Tour" continued through the desert until we arrived at our final destination and the climax of our journey—Israel. The barrenness was behind us as we enjoyed seeing plants, trees, and water again. But being physically present in the locations of the Exodus had helped me better realize how the Israelites' journey has a spiritual parallel for us. As God saved His people from the slavery of Egypt, so too God has saved us from slavery to sin through Jesus Christ. As God supernaturally delivered His people from certain death into new life at the Red Sea by defeating their enemies, so too God has supernaturally given us new life in Jesus Christ by defeating death itself. As God was present with His people as He led them through the desert to their promised land, so too God is present with us as He leads us through this life until we reach our forever home with Him.

Even though we're on our desert journey now, it doesn't have to be a place of bleakness and blandness. God is not at a distance, waiting for us to get to Him. Even now He is close. We have the privilege of seeing the beauty of God and showcasing it to our fellow desert-wanderers as we inch closer to our final destination.

IN HIS IMAGE

Intrinsic in every human soul is the desire to create. We are, after all, made in His image. In some way, shape, or form, every one of us desires to create something beautiful—gardens, food, music, businesses, paintings, for example. Whether it is seen by many or few (or even no one), there is soul-satisfaction in adding beauty to the world.

Just as God, the ultimate Artist, made beauty a priority in His work of Creation, we too share in this holy privilege. As the people of God, we get to model for the world how beautiful the gospel is. Beauty travels farther than words. It needs no translation. It knows no borders. The beauty we create can draw people into His Presence long after our life has ended.

What you, dear artist, create is important. It's more important than you probably realize. The beauty of God, beauty that you have seen and that shapes your work, is the beauty that the desert—and all who journey here—needs. To this end, I pray this book of devotionals is a blessing to you in your creative journey, that it serves you as you welcome God into your creative process and spend time in devotional creativity. In doing so, may it guide you to glimpses of God. May it lead you to create from what you see. May it be for you a path that leads you closer to Him—a path of beauty.

How to Use this Book

BY CATH BUTLER

Imagine yourself standing at the start of a path...

Take a few minutes to notice your surroundings. Perhaps it's a hidden woodland trail, a boot-worn mountain ridge, or paving stones carefully set into trim grass. Allow your anticipation to rise as you imagine what lies ahead—the hidden discoveries, the breathtaking views, the unexpected twists and turns, the eventual arrival. What might it require of you, this journey you're about to undertake? Where might it lead you, how might it shape you? Give some space to acknowledge how you feel as you prepare to step out.

As I picture you on the threshold of departure, I am filled with excitement about how God might use this devotional in the next leg of your journey as one of His artists. Our heart in shaping its content has been that it would facilitate deepening spiritual formation that would, in turn, give rise to overflowing creative expression—

authenticity fuelling the fire of your heart so that your life and work can't help but be marked by its flames.

Or, think of the chapters ahead as being like a midwife accompanying you through the sometimes joyful, sometimes painful process of gestation, labour, and birth that is needed for your inner artist to enter the world... or like an expedition leader helping you to navigate new terrain, notice the places you're passing through, and reach your destination safely.

With that image in mind, there are a few items of "kit" you might want to have to hand for the journey: this book (your route map), a Bible (like a fuller travel guide to refer to), your journal (to record your experiences), and creative materials of your choice for the optional practices (every traveller loves taking photos, so think of this as your artistic equivalent).

Our "route" can be undertaken in a few different ways:

1. For a 21-day journey: read a chapter a day, leaving out the optional reflective and artistic practices, or engaging with them on the same day as one of the numbered chapters.

2. For a four-week journey: read a section each week—a chapter daily for five days, then a day each for the reflective and artistic practises offered at the end of each section. If "life happens" and you end up with only five or six days in a week, you can always skip either or both optional practices. Conclude your final week with Chapter 21.

3. For a month-long journey: like the four-week journey, read a section a week—five days for the chapters plus two days for one or both optional practices. In the last few days of the month, read Chapter 21 and take a day or two to review the journey with a final reflective practice, gathering the graces you've received along the way.

However you approach it, may you know the very Presence of God as your guide and companion, loving and changing you and your creativity, inside and out.

Christ be with me, Christ before me,
Christ behind me, Christ within me,
Christ beneath me, Christ above me,
Christ on my right, Christ on my left,
Christ when I lie down,
Christ when I sit down,
Christ when I arise,
Christ in the heart of every man who thinks of me,
Christ in the mouth of everyone who speaks of me,
Christ in every eye that sees me,
Christ in every ear that hears me.

I arise today through a mighty strength, the invocation of the Trinity,
Through belief in the Threeness, through confession of the Oneness
Of the Creator of creation.

Amen.[1]

---

[1] From St. Patrick's Breastplate

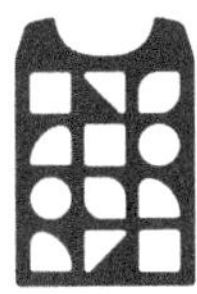

PART ONE:
WALKING WITH OUR CREATOR

"I have come to believe that unless we are making something, we cannot know the depth of God's being and God's grace permeating our lives and God's Creation. Because the God of the Bible is fundamentally and exclusively THE Creator... God cannot be known by sitting in a classroom, or even in a church taking in information about God... The act of Making can lead us to coming to know THE Creator personally..."
—Makoto Fujimura[2]

[2] Makoto Fujimura, *Art + Faith: A Theology of Making*, 2020, Yale University Press, p.7

1. The Secret Place

BY REBECCA BEESE

"There's a heaven on earth that so few ever find, though the map's in your soul and the road's in your mind."
—Dan Fogelberg[3]

Read: Psalm 27:4

Last year I was on a retreat when the Lord spoke to me profoundly about a particularly painful memory. He showed me exactly where He had been in that moment—right there with me. I saw Him in my mind's eye, very clearly, and suddenly that memory wasn't so painful anymore.

As I tend to, I wrote a song about it. Songwriting helps me remember, process, and access deeper emotions, and I didn't want to

---

[3] Dan Fogelberg, *The Wild Places*, The Wild Places, Epic Records, 1990

forget this. I sent the verse and chorus I'd written to three close friends because I wanted to share the beautiful thing that God had done for me—a good motive, right?

On my drive home the next day I was listening to a podcast that told of a professor who got his class to write a poem. They spent the week editing, refining, and reworking until it was as good as they could get it, their very best work. The students arrived back at class, hard work in hand, eager to share the brilliance they'd so carefully crafted. But rather than ask the students to share their creations, the professor got them to rip their poems into tiny pieces, never to be read aloud.

I was horrified.

All that work! That beauty, the message that the world needed to hear and the heart of the artist that needed to be released... gone. The point that the professor was so clearly and so painfully making was the need to create not for the purpose of sharing but for the art itself.

I'd have been devastated.

Yet, in that moment by myself on the road back from Wales, I immediately regretted having shared the song. I felt almost guilty. In my eagerness to share with friends I'd lost something of the precious intimacy Jesus had shown me. I wanted to change the song from what I'd sent, to bring it back to just God and me.

When I arrived home I did just that and decided I'd never share it with anyone. This is a song simply for Jesus and me and, when I play it, I am transported back to that beautiful place with Him. Just us. It is precious because it's ours.

Art, music, poetry, craft... any creative act has two sides to it: the creation, and how it connects with others. We can be so focussed on how it will bring truth, beauty, and life to others that we neglect what the Lord may want to do with us through it. Personally. Devotionally. Relationally. The more connected we are with Him, the more He can reveal to us of who He is and who we are in Him.

But this leads us to ask: is it enough if the only person who sees and values my creativity is God? Is it enough for me to create something for just the two of us? Do I recognise His voice in the noise of the world? Can I discern His leading, even when things are noisy or nasty or falsely resemble goodness? The secret place is where those questions get answered. It's where the pressure comes off and the revelation comes in.

In the context of our busyness and time limitations—we work hard, juggling family and church commitments—time alone with Jesus or to create can feel like an added pressure and potentially something we feel guilty over. I should be doing this... I should be doing that. In a world that often feels time poor, what can we do?

Early in my songwriting journey I heard about Reuben Morgan, who dedicates the best three hours of the day to songwriting. My heart sank. I was a young mum and remember saying to God "...but I don't have three hours a day, let alone three best hours!" God, in His mercy, replied, "I'm not asking that of you—what have you got?" After a bit of thinking I replied, "I could give one evening a month." So, I did. I booked our church hall once a month, not to write songs —just to worship, away from the demands and distractions of home life.

Much of my life has been about preparing for leading others in worship; it's been a danger that I only connect with God when planning something. I've had to be intentional about scheduling time to worship when I'm not preparing or creating, but simply for the pleasure of being with God and to practice hearing and following His voice.

The Lord isn't focussed on our creative outworkings; He wants our hearts. Our creative productions are a wonderful bonus that delight Him, but it's our hearts turned towards Him that is His greatest joy. Time in the secret place is precious, bringing peace to our troubled minds and connection to our lonely souls, rooting us back into all that God is.

APPLICATION

Look at your week and schedule a time for worshipping God in whatever way feels natural to you. The aim is to simply be with God. Don't think beyond the moment. It's almost impossible to be with God and not be inspired creatively, but maybe start a journal or record of things that are just for you and God. Write Him a song that is just for that moment in that room with Him. Create something that you're not going to share beyond those four walls. If you're feeling strong and brave, write Him a poem or create a piece of art that you destroy immediately afterwards, offering it as a sacrifice of worship.

PRAYER

Father God, thank You that You find time with me precious. You love what I do and what I create, but You love me even more. Thank You for the gifts You have given me, thank You for the creative ways I can connect with You. Would You strengthen my connection with You, help me recognise Your voice more clearly, and help me find joy in the secret place with You.

2. Reclaiming Childlike Wonder

BY PETER ASSAD

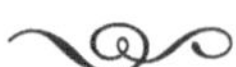

"God delights in the perfect acoustics of ocean waves, swoons over the subtle intensity of dark chocolate, and glories in robins' eggs and peacock calls."
—*Tish Warren*[4]

I realized I was getting older the day I pulled something in my lower back... while sneezing. I wish I was kidding. And it's more than just physical; I feel myself getting older on the inside, too. Somewhere along the way, I've been losing my sense of wonder.

A new restaurant or song used to spark something in me. Lately? It's like I'm cruising through life on autopilot. But my kids are

---

[4] Tish Harrison Warren, *Liturgy of the Ordinary: Sacred Practices in Everyday Life*, 2016, IVP Books, Chapter 10, pp.90-98

an entirely different story! The snail on the sidewalk, the sunlight streaming through the trees, the shadows stretching across the pavement—they notice it all and delight in it.

And so does God.

Think about Jesus of Nazareth, God in human form. He pointed out the birds and lilies, marveled at mustard seeds and fig trees. He paused. He noticed. Even when the world pressed in on Him, He moved unhurried, savoring each moment. Why? Because Jesus doesn't simply show us what God is like—He shows us how to be human again.

When we lose our sense of wonder, we're not just distracted—we're out of sync with the Creator who fashioned a world full of astonishing things, waiting to be seen.

There's a reason Jesus told us we must become like children to enter the Kingdom of Heaven. As adults, we often trade wonder for productivity, mystery for efficiency, delight for duty. But in the Kingdom, wonder isn't a luxury—it's essential. The moment we stop being amazed, we start growing numb.

For artists, wonder is our lifeblood. We're uniquely positioned to lead the way in reclaiming it—not only for ourselves but for the world around us. With a heightened sensitivity to beauty, God has wired us to notice and express what others might overlook. Whether visual, musical, literary, or otherwise, our art offers the world a glimpse into a reality brimming with possibility.

But the journey isn't without its challenges. The constant demands of deadlines, expectations, comparison, and commerce can dull our senses. We may find ourselves distracted, lost in the mechanics of our craft, forgetting why we even began in the first place. We grow tired—or worse, we create out of obligation instead of joy.

Remember, dear artist, you're not just a participant in beauty—you are its interpreter, invited to see what others overlook, so slow down to look with fresh eyes. Your creativity is not just a skill, but a sacred portal that draws others in to glimpse the magnificence woven throughout the world around us.

How can we reclaim and sustain our sense of wonder? How do we ensure that the art we create is not just good work but sacred work—work that honors the beauty of the world and invites others to see it anew?

APPLICATION

- ❖ *Ask for it.*

  Wonder is a gift, not something we manufacture. Our God is a generous Father, giving good gifts to those He loves. If you feel numb to beauty, ask God to reawaken your senses. Ask Him to soften your spirit, lift your gaze, and renew your joy. He delights in answering this kind of prayer.

- ❖ *Pause for it.*

  Our lives are loud and fast. Wonder needs space, so slow down. Turn off the noise. Stop scrolling. Go outside. Linger over your coffee. Let beauty interrupt you. God speaks through sunsets, silence, and leaves that rustle in the breeze. But we'll miss it if we never stop moving.

- ❖ *Engage it.*

  When something stirs your soul, don't just move on. Lean in, and let it turn into a prayer. Journal about it. Sketch it. Sing it. Thank God for it. The more you engage with wonder, the more it enlarges every part of you.

❖ *Share it.*
Wonder is contagious. When something amazes you, share it. Tell a friend. Show your kids. Talk about what moved you. Sharing wonder multiplies joy and invites others into the beauty too.

So keep your eyes open. The world is still brimming with wonder, and your calling is to help the rest of us see it—for the One older than time itself leads the way, and He invites us to follow Him.

PRAYER

God, I confess how easy it is to grow old in the places You've asked me to stay young. I've let the rush of life dull my sense of wonder. Reignite this childlike, Christlike wonder within me again. Help me slow down, breathe deeply, and be surprised by Your goodness—that my wonder would lead me back to worship, and inspire the same in others.

3. Creating From Covenant

BY JIMMY ORR

"But God didn't make a contract with us; God made a covenant with us, and God wants our relationships with one another to reflect that covenant. That's why marriage, friendship, life in community are all ways to give visibility to God's faithfulness in our lives together."

—Henri Nouwen[5]

I was once a busker[6] on the London Underground.

Auditioned before a judging panel in a disused part of Charing Cross station, I got my licence and sang cover songs at unsuspecting, subterranean members of the public. I absolutely loved it! I met some fun people, learned to play and sing better, and made a bit of money

---

[5] Henri Nouwen, *Bread for the Journey: A Daybook of Wisdom and Faith*, 1996, Harper Collins, March 2

[6] A busker is "a person who performs music or other entertainment in the street or another public place for monetary donations" (Oxford Languages).

too. It was a thoroughly enjoyable way to pass a couple of hours a few times a week... until I moved out of London.

I moved to stay with my Mum and Dad for a while but continued busking on the Tube. Except now, to make it worth my while, I had to at least earn my train fare to and from London. I didn't want to pay to busk! As soon as I felt the need to make money, the enjoyment level plummeted. It became a job. I started singing the songs I knew commuters would give their change for, and not songs I just liked playing.

That is the difference between covenant and contract.

A contract is an exchange of goods or services. You work X number of hours for me; I pay you Y amount of money. For this much per month you will receive these channels, this loan, so much data, or access to that.

A covenant is relational; a giving of oneself to another. In sickness and in health, till death parts us. Nothing can separate us.[7] Creating for the sheer pleasure of creating.

Jesus told His followers, "I do not call you servants any longer, because the servant does not know what the master is doing; but I have called you friends, because I have made known to you everything that I have heard from my Father" (Jn. 15:15, NRSV).

"The Lord confides in those who fear Him;
He makes His covenant known to them" (Ps. 25:14).

We don't confide in just anybody. We tend to confide only in those we love and trust. So, for God to confide in someone is to say God deeply loves that person and trusts them, and that person is *you.*

---

7 Romans 8:31-39

Imagine that! God loves you enough to draw near, stooping down and getting close enough to whisper into your ear, "Hey, this is what I'm thinking, and I want to share it with you."

We are not commissioned to make art in exchange for some reward or blessing. Making art *is* the blessing! We are in relationship with the Artist and, as such, we are invited to co-create with Him as an expression and outworking of that relationship. We don't create from a place of contract; we create from a place of covenant. Out of the overflow of the heart the mouth speaks.[8]

When we create from the security of that unconditional love, it produces an honesty that simply cannot be fabricated. You produce your most authentic art when you are at your most authentic—and that is the art that speaks most to people.

The most honest artists I know are my kids. They draw, they paint, they craft, they stick (so much glitter)! I love watching them in the moment as their imaginations go wild and they're in full flow, and out of the chaos and carnage of the materials and mess comes their creation. It's not necessarily going to win any critics' award or public acclaim, but it's honest, it's imaginative, it's theirs, and I love it. For a few days it takes pride of place displayed on the fridge, which everyone knows is the Louvre of any family home!

Jesus calls us to be like little children. Maybe this is some of what He means—to be so safe and secure in our Father's love that we feel free to create what we want to create. Not what we think people will like. Not what might earn us likes or money. Not even what we think we ought to paint or sing or show. No, we get lost in the wonder of the process and imaginatively express something of our authentic selves. If other people see or hear or experience it, great!

---

[8] Luke 6:45

I'm sure they will connect with your honesty and vulnerability in a deep, personal way (and if they don't, that's not your problem). But God will take that creativity, honour your intentions and your honesty, and with divine and fatherly pride add your piece to the great fridge door in the heavens saying, "My child did that! I love it, and I love them!"

APPLICATION

Think about what you would create if you knew it would never be judged... and then do it! In other words, create like a kid again. If you're a painter, grab some simple primary colours and mix them together in that beautifully basic way. Get stuck in with finger-painting! If you like crafting, build a sculpture out of recycling and glitter! If you like writing poems or songs, use the most unorthodox and out-of-this-world imagery. Or maybe it's as simple as putting on the music, turning it up loud, and dancing like nobody's watching. Enjoy the process!

PRAYER

Father—what a miracle that we have the privilege of calling You that! We are eternally grateful that You have called us to be Your children and blessed us with the family trait of creativity. Help us to express these gifts with childlike freedom—releasing art into Your world that is authentic and honest and rooted in the awesome covenantal love between us. In Your name and for Your glory. Amen.

4. Trinity, Creation, and the Artist

BY HUNTER LYNCH

"The first fact about the man 'made in the image of God' is that he was created to create, as God creates... The characteristic common to God and man is apparently that: the desire and the ability to make things."
—Dorothy L. Sayers[9]

In very specific language, the book of Genesis gives the reader a glance at the triune God at work—every person within the Godhead in full, undivided operation. We see the Spirit hovering upon the waters. We see the very Word of God causing all things to be and to remain. Speaking within Triune community, God creates humanity. At the foundation of all creative effort lies the God of the Universe, the

---

[9] Dorothy L. Sayers, *The Mind of the Maker*, 1941, Harcourt, Brace, p.17

Unmade Maker. All artistry is God's, though it is often implemented for purposes antithetical to its very reason for being. So what are we called to do, as a people set apart to create for the Creator? As followers of Jesus, a redeemed people who are expected to imitate the One who made us, I believe we should ask the question: how do the persons of the Godhead serve as a guiding light for the artist?

Let us first look to the Father, the Giver of all good things. He is the great, unseen God who has formed all that we see and enjoy according to His perfect wisdom and goodness. We would be foolish to ignore the joy that our Father expresses when deeming His creation "good." As creating believers, we typically find ourselves within the suffocating cycle of constantly second-guessing our motives, or abilities, and even our calling. We are certainly in a much bigger hurry to deem things "BAD," be that directed at our own efforts or at the newest CCM equivalent to a pre-teen Justin Bieber. Our overly-critical spirits are symptomatic of a grace deficiency towards ourselves and our brothers and sisters in Christ. Yes, there are times for humility and introspection, to be sure, but if we are to mirror our Father in heaven we must have grace towards our own works, as well as the works of others, so that we may partake in the goodness of completed creation. The Father began with the formless, void canvas and filled it with beauty. We would do well to take the empty page, canvas, or Google Doc and bring good things into being.

Now, we consider the Son: the Image of the Invisible God. It is plain to us that God saw fit to take on real, physical flesh and walk among us on the dust of His own making. In the Incarnation the Invisible is made visible, the Mystery is made man. In a very similar but not directly comparable way we do this as artists. In this process of creating from nothing we give form to the formless whimsy of the mind. We jot down the melody that flies into focus for a brief, fleeting moment and seek to pin its wings down before it goes. Or we miss it in front of the Starbucks barista and do our best not to cry into a drink we were embarrassed to order out loud. Truly, the spontaneous, explosive nature of a moment of inspiration is like nothing else on earth. It's something unique to the artist that is difficult to put into words, but you know it when it happens. It is our job to take those electric moments and turn them into monuments for everyone to see. Time and time again, I have woken from a dream where a specific melody is playing in the background. It's quite easy to go back to sleep and forget it ever happened, but I've made the habit of quietly (for my poor wife's sake) recording a voice memo before I turn over, just in case something useful is there. Artists live in this space of pulling from our world, our experiences, and our voices, and creating something finite and observable. This is a very small way in which we shadow the physical nature of the Son, yet it is nonetheless emboldening in our pursuit of creating with our whole being. It is through these means that we bring praise to Emmanuel, the God-man who wrote Himself into the grand narrative of creation.

Lastly, let us ponder the role of the Spirit in the life of the artist. Certainly, under the gift of general revelation, humans can create without considering the Giver of the gift. However, as Christians our meager efforts are sanctified and led by the power of the Holy Spirit. The Spirit is the guiding force behind all meaningful and good creative labors. John 16:13 says: "But when He, the Spirit of truth, comes, He will guide you into all the truth. He will not speak on His own, but will speak whatever He hears, and He will tell you what is yet to come." Apart from the Spirit the artist has no hope of glorifying God, therefore submission to the guiding work of the Spirit should be our golden standard. This works out in the way that we co-write with others, seeing one another as image-bearers and not as image-taking enemies, as some tense writing sessions are prone to cause us to believe. Being led by the Spirit in that context means seeking unity as is commanded by our Savior. It means resisting the urge to reach across the table to throw a stale donut with the intent to kill! Additionally, submitting to the Spirit's lead works out in how we kneel to God's Word over our own creative vision. Maybe there's a line we're married to that isn't theologically clear. Maybe there are extra-biblical assumptions made that aren't grounded in historically-backed research. Above all, the peace-giving, truth-leading Presence of the Spirit should guide our creative process, or we will quickly find ourselves as the builders of Babel: left in a mixture of confusion and pointless creation. Instead, let our aim be complete submission to the slow work of the Spirit, guiding us into peace-governed creation that elevates the name of the Creator.

APPLICATION

- ❖ What are some practical ways that you can more proactively "pin down" those moments in which you are inspired to create? What kind of parachutes can you give yourself so you don't miss it?
- ❖ Think about the last few projects you've been a part of. Looking back, can you see more clearly now how the Trinity was present in your labor?
- ❖ Moving forward, what are some creative pitfalls you can be more mindful of, where you need the strength of the Spirit to navigate and overcome?
- ❖ Spend time in personal prayer, resting in the fact that God is not rushing you through the task at hand, nor are His

affections tied to how well it turns out! Thank Him for the simple gift of the invitation to create alongside Him.

PRAYER

Father, I ask You today to order every effort, not only in my speech and actions but specifically in all I seek to create. Grant me grace for those I seek to partner with so that in collaborative unity You might be glorified. Help me to let go of any well-loved lyric (or artistic detail) that may present itself as an impediment beneath the chisel of critique. May I find true joy in the calling You have placed upon my life to strengthen Your Church through the gift and glory of the arts. Let this work make much of the name of Jesus, and may I be content in Your favor when the praise of man is lacking. For within that silence Your approval is most known, and can provide ample nourishment to the soul that is starved for affirmation. Author of all good beginnings, bring this work to its completion as I submit to Your Spirit's prompting. Amen.

5. Stones of Remembrance

BY CATHERINE & HENRY MILLER

"Remember the wonders He has done, His miracles, and the judgments He pronounced..."
—Psalm 105:5a

Read: Joshua 4

On a warm day in July, our hand-me-down blue Honda Pilot sputtered to a halt on the side of the road in a food desert half an hour from home. I was minutes away from art camp with my three children in tow, no food or water, in a city unfamiliar to me. Fighting anxiety, fear, and panic, we worked to remember the stories of the Israelites. I pulled out the camping chairs and opened the trunk, and waited for the tow truck and my husband to come get us.

As we waited, God was with us. Three strangers stopped to give us snacks and water, and one guy even tried to fix it for us. But this was just the beginning. The short version is, that day in the food desert ushered in a season of wilderness for our family as we learned to bring our lives into order with God's Word. This was a painful season of God's testing and healing our trauma, and learning to let the Lord tangibly provide for us our daily bread. The night we wrestled with our financial situation, Henry felt that God was telling us to write a song. This evening of groaning birthed *The Provision Song*, based on Psalm 77. Every time we struggled with doubt that God would provide, we sang that song to remind us of what He had done. Singing the song gave us strength and later provided testimony as we shared it with others.

Our song, *Lead Me to the Water*, is another "memorial stone." The first verse is an honest cry from my heart two years ago as God led me into a wilderness season of learning to trust and obey Him.

> *If you heal the broken pieces of my soul*
> *Who would I become? Where might I go?*
> *If you lead me to the water, will I run?*
> *Will I hide my face? Or will I follow?*

I remember the morning I penned those words. The melody flowed from my heart as I wrestled with my emotions. Like the Israelites, I struggled to trust God. I wanted to follow Jesus with the boldness of Paul, but I forgot about the three-year period of transformation that came before he began his ministry.[10] The song continues with a chorus:

---

[10] Galatians 1:18

Lead me to the water,
May I thirst no more;
Heal my heart, Lord:
Bring healing to my soul.

The Israelites' journey traces a winding path from Egypt to Canaan as they follow the pillar of cloud. And sometimes, the cloud stops.

If we examine the path with left-brain logic it doesn't seem to make sense. Why would Yahweh lead the nation through such a twisting, indirect route? Yet the wilderness is not simply a path between two points for the Israelites, but a liminal space. Liminal comes from the Latin *limen* meaning "threshold"—a space between spaces—and so the wilderness is a journey of the nation of Israel leaving the pain and trauma of Egypt behind them and integrating their story with God's story. (How far will God take us to integrate our stories with His?!) It is in the wilderness that they meet Yahweh's holy Presence in the beauty of tabernacle worship, and depend on the Lord to provide for their physical needs of food and water. Miraculously, their clothes and sandals do not wear out along the journey either! As they journey in liminal space, they find the healing and restoration from the living water they have needed all along. Joining Yahweh in His work of constructing the tabernacle, they learn what it means to worship God.

In Joshua 4, Israel finally exits the wilderness and crosses the Jordan River into Canaan. Joshua follows God's command to set up 12 stones from the Jordan as a memorial to how God delivered His people. Joshua tells the Israelites that when their children ask what the stones mean, to tell them that "'Israel crossed the Jordan on dry ground... so that all the peoples of the earth might know that the hand of the LORD is powerful and so that you might always fear the LORD your God'" (v.22-24).

We wrote these songs in response to dark places in our present and our past. When I share our songs now, I testify to what God has done in our lives. They are "memorial stones" for us and encouragement for others. They have become a catalyst for people to encounter and remember God.

APPLICATION

Write about a time when God delivered you, healed you, or encouraged you. As you do, be honest about the darkness or difficult circumstances that required your deliverance. Commit to incorporating your honest reactions to such darkness into your work as a spiritual discipline—and commit to incorporating your honest reactions to God's light entering into those dark places.

PRAYER

Lord, You meet me in the wilderness—with water, with strangers, and songs. Lead me as You led Your people through dry places. Remind me of Your faithfulness. Help me carry these memories like stones of remembrance—testimonies of Your provision and healing. Whenever (lie/habit—name it)* arises, strengthen me to go where You go and stay where You stay, till all my stories reflect Your glory and invite others to trust You. Amen.

*The journey through the wilderness can bring up stuff from your past that's keeping you from moving forward: with your art, your relationships, and your life. When you notice these habits and beliefs, you can name them in this prayer.

Reflective & Artistic Practices

BY NANCY NETHERCOTT

"O Lord, You who are the Creator of heaven and earth, may we take pleasure in Your creation this day as You take pleasure in it, we pray, and may we live this day as a people who have been crowned with glory, so that all we do may be done in praise of You and in anticipation of that day when the whole world shall be made fully and forever alive. We pray this in the name of the One who makes heaven and earth for love's sake. Amen."
—W. David O. Taylor[11]

PART 1: FOR TAKING PLEASURE IN GOD'S CREATION

The Presence and beauty of our Creator God—Father, Son, and Holy Spirit—is all around us every single day. Do we notice? Are we paying attention? How can we cultivate awareness and be meaningfully present to God and the world around us?

The title of this section gives us a hint: walk! As holistic beings, engaging our bodies actually helps open our minds and hearts to God.

---

[11] W. David O. Taylor, *Prayers for the Pilgrimage: A Book of Collects for All of Life*, 2024, IVP, p.187

Over the next two days, reflect on the previous devotional chapters as you walk outside in nature. Take in the overarching breadth of how God has been speaking to you, or dive deeper with one word that moved you. Find an area that "speaks" to you, where you can hear God's voice and attune to the inner movements of your heart. Maybe a walk on the beach, or in the woods, or in a nature preserve, or in the mountains. It might be in the daytime, or at night to view the wonder of the stars or Northern Lights, or both—you might want to take multiple walks! Possibly, one walking path is in a sort of "secret garden" for reflecting on Chapter 1.

As you walk, engage your senses. Notice what you hear, smell, feel. Then, consider:

- ❖ What does God want to say to you as you walk in silence and solitude with your Creator?
- ❖ Is there restoration for your body, mind, and soul as you walk and process?

Let today be about noticing. You might record a few thoughts or images in a journal to return to later.

PART 2: FOR RESPONDING CREATIVELY

Having engaged in your reflective practice of walking with the Creator, let's move from simply noticing to responding. These walks are not just about observation, but deepening our experience with God through presence, listening, and creative expression.

As you recall your walking and review any thoughts or images you recorded, ask yourself:

- ❖ How do you feel invited to respond?

❖ Is there a way you feel led to express gratitude, awe, and wonder?

❖ What might you create as a means of response?

Whether through words, music, movement, drawing, photography, or another medium entirely, take time now to respond from a place of connection with your Creator. Let it be honest. Let it be joyful. Let it be worship.

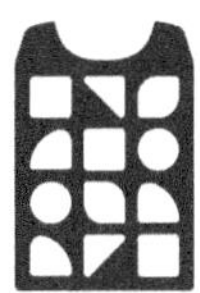

PART TWO:
WALKING WITH OUR CALLING

"Calling is not only a matter of being and doing what we are but also of becoming what we are not yet but are called by God to be."
—Os Guiness[12]

[12] Os Guiness, *The Call: Finding and Fulfilling the Central Purpose of Your Life*, 1998, Word, p.30

6. What is an Artist?

BY CAMERON MILLER

"Your true identity is a gift of God, a surprising discovery, and then a committed choice."
—David Powlison[13]

What defines an artist? The obvious answer is that they're someone who creates art. But in talking with God, I'm starting to get a deeper picture of what being an artist entails.

I believe an artist is first and foremost a person of vision. They see a picture in their head, something no one else can see, something that isn't yet but should be. I'm not just talking about eyesight—I'm referring to any of the senses, especially those we don't have names for yet. Your "vision" could be the beginnings of a melody, an idea for

---

[13] David Powlinson, *ESV Men's Devotional Bible*, 2015, Crossway

a story, a concept for a new dish, or even a new way of living that breaks from old patterns of failure.

Artists are not content to hoard vision to themselves. It must be shared. They use any tools they can to communicate this vision so that others can see it with the same clarity. We have a name for these tools: art. Art has the power to allow another person to imagine what was previously only in the artist's head. By this definition, the amount of art you create doesn't determine how much of an artist you are. Instead, you are an artist because God planted a seed deep in your soul that no one can kill or destroy. You can cultivate that seed as you grow your artistic gift. Hardship may slow it, but God's purposes will be achieved. You will improve at expressing the vision inside you, but also become able to envision with greater clarity. To that end, you'll never be able to fully express what you see this side of heaven. Such is the artist's struggle.

One of the things artists do is create beauty. God made the world good and gave it to us like a parent giving art supplies to a child. Beauty can be a collage that pleases the eyes, music that pleases the ears, a recipe that pleases the tongue, or even a story that pleases the mind.

Art can also reveal truth. Scientists search for truth in things that can be quantified, controlled, and calculated. But we artists search out realities so far beyond us that they can't be reasoned out by a limited mind, yet not so abstract that they can't be glimpsed by a sensitive heart. With beauty, we draw people to consider truths they would otherwise not face, and with truth, we reveal the beauty of things others might take for granted.

As Christians, we have a special privilege: to see into the heavenly realm and share what we find. My hunch is that God selects artists to be His modern-day prophets. It's not because He needs us to get His message across, but our artist hearts long to say something that has meaning, so He gives us something meaningful to say. If I'm right about this, Amos 3:7 is all the more exciting: "Surely the Sovereign LORD does nothing without revealing His plan to His servants the prophets." That would mean that when God's about to do something, He gets the word out through His artists, and if you want to know what's coming next, just look at what His servants are creating.

Beyond that, I think every work of art is prophetic in some way, because prophecy is about communicating God's message and heart to a people distant from Him. For me, sometimes that looks like the Holy Spirit bringing me recipe ideas in my dreams. How does a delicious dessert pizza move forward the gospel and accomplish God's purposes on this earth? I have no idea. And I don't need to. Artists function as watchers on the walls, positioned to allow them to see further and clearer than those on the ground. And it is their duty to report what they see. If what I see is a circle of sweetbread topped with pie filling and frosted, that is what I bake, and I trust God with the results. There's nothing too small for Him to use according to His purposes.

As artists we have the vision to create what otherwise would not exist. We are gifted to make beauty out of chaos and proclaim truth to the doubter. From a right relationship with God, we are given His messages to convey with whatever skill we possess. There are other callings in the Kingdom, but this is ours, and I wouldn't trade mine for anything else.

APPLICATION

Set aside some time this week to bring an inner vision to creative reality. As you do so, talk with God about how you see yourself as an artist.

PRAYER

Lord, You have placed vision in me—a seed only You can grow. When I doubt my worth as an artist and question the gifts You've given me to carry, remind me that obedience matters more than output. Open my eyes to see what others miss and make me bold to create what only I can—speaking beauty that reveals truth, and truth that reveals beauty. Like a prophet on the wall, may I watch with wonder and create with trust, knowing You will use every piece of it for Your glory and our good. Amen.

7. What is Beauty?

BY JOHN ELKINS

"In the beginning, God created the heavens and the earth. The earth was without form and void, and darkness was over the face of the deep. And the Spirit of God was hovering over the face of the waters."
—*Genesis 1:1-2 (ESV)*

Arriving before the police, I was the first on the scene to be with the family. I sat for hours, offering counsel and presence. I wept with my friend's grieving wife and children, offering them the only hope I know—the love of Jesus for them through me. I had no words to give, only the presence of a fellow suffering brother who loved their family deeply.

Faced with the empty ugliness of my friend's suicide, I spent the next month creating. I wrote poems, painted pictures in honor of my friend, and published books. When I gave the book of poetry and art to his son, he felt loved and began to write his own poetry, because creative-beauty is contagious. When I revealed my heart in the artwork I presented to his wife and daughter, the wife began to find healing in sharing her hurts with the community and she let herself be revealed through opportunities to paint.

Artistic expression serves us in such difficulties. Creativity gives form and shape to that which was void and empty, often providing a sense of meaning amidst pain. Beauty brings light into the soul's darkness, life to dead spaces, and love into sharp focus in a blurry world.

Consider the creation and creativity of God.

God began creation out of nothing. Bringing beauty of life into emptiness. Emptiness. Not ugliness. A life without beauty is emptiness. Beauty is the defiance of emptiness. Without life, there is no beauty. Without beauty, there is only emptiness and formlessness. All beauty is found in life and victory over the empty formlessness.

BEAUTY IS GOD'S DEFINING, LIFE-BRINGING PRESENCE

Darkness hovered over the great unknown-deep. The "deep" is a term used in the Bible to refer to the sea and the creatures therein, evoking fear and terror.[14] The author of Genesis compounds that terrifying image with the emptiness of darkness hovering over it. But notice, when God enters the scene the darkness is replaced by "the Spirit of God" and "the deep" becomes "waters." When God is present darkness flees, and that which is terrifyingly unknown becomes defined and majestic. The same truth is presented in Jesus'

---

[14] Genesis 7:11, 8:2; Job 38:30; Psalm 36:6, 42:7, 69:15; Isaiah 44:27, 51:10; Amos 7:4

appearance in John 1 when the divine *Logos* enters the world and darkness cannot overcome it.[15]

BEAUTY IS REVEALED IN AND THROUGH THE LIGHT

By nature, light exposes. In a world without light no one can see the beauty of life. Like emptiness, darkness veils beauty. But light brings beauty into existence. As long as beauty remains in the dark it cannot be taken in and therefore cannot fully exist.

When Jesus comes to earth, the definition and majesty of creation are reinvigorated and restored to the glory of the garden paradise in Him. He is God displayed for all to see—the perfect image of God on the canvas of life, recreating the souls of men into the beautiful image-bearers intended. Moreover, He is the "light of life" and the life of all mankind so that men CAN see.[16] In His light, and only in Him, humanity is capable of seeing true beauty.

BEAUTY IS LOVE

In the first garden, Adam and Eve were tasked with expanding the beauty of God's image across the earth.[17] Our commission remains the same. The people of God are to strive to cultivate beauty in their every act of being. We mimic the creative process of God when we lay form and definition on canvas. We mimic the beauty of God's *Logos* when we bring harmony and melody together in polyphonic productions of music and reveal the great love of our King.

---

[15] John 1:5

[16] John 1:4-5, 9-13

[17] Genesis 1:26

For all our creative efforts to produce beauty, we find beauty most clearly displayed in Christ's love for us. That love that bends to the earth to give form to the void.[18] That beautiful forgiveness that kneels down to the earth to draw in the dirt.[19] That wonderful grace that humbles itself to wash the feet of the disciples, even the murderer.[20]

That same beautiful love is given to us to give to others. Jesus tells us that the world will know us by our love.[21] Our greatest display of beauty is the act of love. Love that brings form to void. Love that brings life to emptiness. Love that dies to self to see others come alive. Love that sits and mourns with the family after a death. Love that holds the hands of the bereaved. Love that labors to produce art that could bring hope into hopelessness. The love of Christ poured out through His people. It is this love that is the foundation of beauty.

So, strive to cultivate beauty in all of life, enjoying the character of God and sharing His love with everyone. Create art, music, and literature that reflects God's own glorious act of love-wrought beauty. Serve in the dirt to re-write the souls of men with the truth that Jesus has freed us from all sin and raised us to resurrected life. Be a people marked by the beauty of the gospel of Jesus Christ, as it is written: "How beautiful upon the mountains are the feet of him who brings good news, who publishes peace, who brings good news of happiness, who publishes salvation, who says to Zion, 'Your God reigns'" (Is. 52:7, ESV).

---

[18] Genesis 1:1-2, John 1:1-5

[19] John 7:53-8:10

[20] John 13

[21] John 13:35

APPLICATION

Can you remember a time of darkness or emptiness in your own life? A time when all things seemed empty and void? We all have dark moments—the passing of a father, rejection from a friend, the death of a dream, or failing in a career. We all deal with dark-dreadful moments and struggle to find joy or meaning at times in life. Art is appointed to answer such moments. Painting, poetry, music, a well-prepared meal, the cultivation of a garden, the arranging of furniture in a well-used room, whatever expression a person can muster, we meet emptiness with beauty.

How can you, as an artist, bring form, definition, and life to something previously undefined, chaotic, or empty? Is there a specific project or work you could produce to reflect the glory of God and bring beauty to emptiness?

In what ways can you serve as a light that reveals the beauty of Jesus to the world around you? How has God called you to use your creative work to accomplish this?

How can you use your creative gifts to bring beauty and love to the world around you?

PRAYER

Lord of Life, I long to join in Your creative work. As an image-bearer, I long to reflect the love that You display to all people—to see beauty spring from the souls of believers who have been brought from death to life in Jesus. Inspire my heart and mind to creative expression. Help me to display Your glory and grace to the world around me. I love You. I trust You. Accomplish Your will in me. Amen.

8. A Beautiful Waste

by Peter Assad

"Aware of this, Jesus said to them, 'Why are you bothering this woman? She has done a beautiful thing to me.'"
—*Matthew 26:10*

It takes time to create—to hone our craft, be inspired, chase it down, refine (and refine again), grow disillusioned, shelve it for a while, then eventually return, half-convinced it might someday hang next to the *Mona Lisa*. Yet whenever we try to give ourselves the space and grace to create, the question undoubtedly comes up: is any of this worth it?

In Matthew 26, Jesus is at a dinner party with His disciples when a woman shows up and makes a scene. She brings an alabaster jar of perfume and cracks it open to anoint the head of Jesus. Scandalous. Verses 8–9 depict the outrage: "When the disciples saw this, they were indignant. 'Why this waste?' they asked. 'This perfume could have been sold at a high price and the money given to the poor.'"

According to Mark's gospel account of this story, the perfume was worth 300 denarii (a denarius is a day's wage). That's roughly a year's salary—what a staggering cost! And not just in money, but in time. Is there anything worse than wasting our own time? "Why this waste?" they protest, because just like that, one whole year was lost. Or was it?

How interesting Jesus' response is—what she's done is "a beautiful thing." In fact, this act of waste is an offering that mirrors the beauty of God's creation. Just like He gazed at the world and declared it good, this woman's act of pouring out her most valuable possessions—her time, her resources—is a beautiful reflection of God's creativity. It's a reminder that what we do, when done with intentionality and love, can be a beautiful offering.

Of course Jesus would see this! Of course it'd be God to know and name and prioritize and define what is beautiful. But when He calls something beautiful, He's not just making a general statement. He's pointing to an act that reflects His heart—whether it's a woman's sacrificial gift of perfume or the creative work we do when we reflect His image. Beauty, in God's eyes, is often about intentionality, purpose, and sacrifice.

Quick example from the Old Testament, all the way back to creation in Genesis. After each act of forging, forming, and filling this world, God declared it all "good."[22] We may hear the word "good" and think something along the lines of "adequate" or "good job," but the Hebrew word here is *tov* (which means a lot more than just "good"). A few chapters later, we get a clue as this same word is used to describe

---

[22] Genesis 1:4, 10, 12, 18, 21, 25, 31

a woman named Rebekah, saying she was "very beautiful *(tov)*."[23] "Big deal," you say? Try calling someone you love "adequate" and tell me how that goes.

When God creates all we see around us, He's not some manager checking off His to-do list. No, He's the four-year-old child looking up to find a sky filled with cotton-candy clouds, exclaiming, "Wow!" He's the grandmother in the delivery room with her daughter, dumbfoundedly watching as this precious newborn emerges into the world. He's the groom at the altar—tears welling up in His eyes as His bride makes her way down the aisle: "Beautiful... beautiful... it's all so beautiful."

Think of all the intricate designs in creation—the stars that sing millions and billions of light years away. Consider the way an eagle can ascend and glide into the heavens without a single flap of its wing, or the way the carbon dioxide we exhale, which would kill us, feeds the trees and gets recycled into oxygen again for us. It's good. It's *tov*. It's beautiful.

This same pursuit of beauty is our birthright, because Jesus not only understands beauty but savors and celebrates it. And because we are made in the image of this Creator God, our own acts of creation —whether big or small—carry that same potential for beauty. When we create, we tap into the divine, mirroring God's work in the world.

Allow Him to silence the naysayers, those voices of doubt or scorn that try to diminish the worth of your work. It's easy to listen to the critics, whether internal or external, but what you're doing— when it's poured out in alignment with God's purpose—is beautiful. Don't let anyone convince you otherwise. Hear Him invite you and

---

[23] Genesis 24:16

encourage you with these words, because what you are doing is a beautiful thing.

APPLICATION

If you believed with every fiber of your being that what Jesus says about how you spend your time for Him is beautiful, how might that change your approach to creativity?

PRAYER

Lord, help me believe what You say and no one else, to the point that I'm no longer swayed internally by a compliment that goes to my head or a criticism that goes to my heart. May the time I spend creating be a beautiful thing because it is meant for You.

9. Remade in the Making

BY CATH BUTLER

"The very first step is to try to forget about the self altogether. Your real, new self (which is Christ's and also yours, and yours just because it is His) will not come as long as you are looking for it. It will come when you are looking for Him... Give up your self, and you will find your real self. Lose your life and you will save it. Submit to death, death of your ambitions and favourite wishes every day and death of your whole body in the end: submit with every fibre of your being, and you will find eternal life. Keep back nothing. Nothing that you have not given away will ever be really yours. Nothing in you that has not died will ever be raised from the dead. Look for yourself, and you will find in the long run only hatred, loneliness, despair, rage, ruin, and decay. But look for Christ and you will find Him, and with Him everything else thrown in."

—C.S. Lewis[24]

---

[24] C.S. Lewis, *Mere Christianity*, 1996, Touchstone, pp.190-191

Read: John 12:20-28

Let me start with a question: what if our creativity is one of the primary arenas in which our discipleship takes place? If you're anything like me, it's all too easy to keep the categories of "artist" and "disciple" in different boxes—to think of creativity in terms of doing over being, product over person. Say "creativity" and my thoughts tend towards the art I make, and maybe its future, more than what my Maker might be wanting to make in me.

But what if we joined those boxes up and allowed them to influence each other? What if our making could be a place where we learn more about our Maker: what He's like, what He loves, how He works, what He wants? What if it could be a place where we allow Him to shape and form us in the depths of our being—our hearts, desires, dreams, hopes—even as we shape and form our art in the exercise of our craft? What if it could be a place where we learn what it means for us to follow Him? And what if all that rippled out into how we live the rest of our lives?

Perhaps you have already experienced this interweaving of creativity and discipleship in your life: moments of sheer joy and exhilaration in the creative process when you know you've glimpsed a little of God's delight in making you and all you see... times when you can't settle or sleep because there's one word in one line, or one brushstroke in one section, that isn't sitting right—and you find yourself reflecting on the careful intentionality and thoughtful attention to detail God gives to every aspect of His design. At the moment, thanks to the iron-sharpening-iron beauty of creative community, God is using my song writing journey to make me acutely aware of how reluctant I am to share myself. I am aware of His gentle invitation to walk back through the years with Him, noticing when and where my natural creative sharing was stifled, allowing Him to show me how He was present in those moments, and receiving the healing and perspective He wants to offer. He'll go as deep as exchanging my view of myself for His, if I let Him. There's an opportunity for me to hand my fears over to Him, to confess my temptations to creative self-sabotage, to choose to come out of hiding, and accept His call, crying out to Him for the courage to follow through on that. All this if I will simply pay attention to how He is discipling me through my creativity.

This isn't just about processing our personal journey through the art we make; it's deeper and richer and more wonder-full than that. Processing through our art is part of it, but beyond that it is about sucking all the goodness from the discipleship feast placed before us in our creative practice, reorientating from product to person, learning to notice and respond to the discipleship gifts and invitations—to know, love, and serve Him—that God offers us in and through our creativity.

But here's the rub: when we are following Jesus, discipleship is (often) a downward path. It's the way of the seed that falls to the ground and dies before there can be a harvest,[25] of the bread that gets blessed and broken in the process of being multiplied[26] ... it's the way of the cross. Discipleship is the lifelong process of losing our lives to truly find them, of following the One who, "although being in very nature the Creator, did not consider equality with the Creator (never mind creative success) something to be grasped, but made Himself nothing, taking on the form of a slave, being born in human likeness. And being found in human form, He humbled Himself and became

---

[25] John 12:24-25

[26] Matthew 14:13-21

obedient to the point of death—even death on a cross" (Phil. 2:6-8, adapted). So, if our own creative "way" doesn't involve sacrifice and dying to ourselves somehow, mightn't there be something wrong?

Yes, Jesus laid down His life to take it up again,[27] and yes, there are seasons of birthing and ministering and resurrection life as well as of dying—we need to live into the length and breadth and height and depth of Jesus' story in our creative discipleship. But here's the heart of it: our creativity must change us before it can change the world.

APPLICATION

How is your discipleship impacting your creativity? How is your creativity influencing your discipleship? Reflect on your creative journey to date: can you see some of the discipleship gifts and invitations God has held out to you through it in different seasons? What about right now?

PRAYER

Jesus, thank You so much for giving me creativity as a place of discipleship. Help me to notice and respond openly and joyfully to the gifts and invitations You offer me through it, allowing You—my Creator—to continue to create me in my deepest parts.

---

[27] John 10:17

10. The Artist's Conscience

BY ELISE MASSA

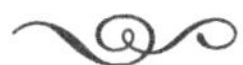

"And you, my son Solomon, acknowledge the God of your father, and serve Him with wholehearted devotion and with a willing mind, for the Lord searches every heart and understands every desire and every thought. If you seek Him, He will be found by you; but if you forsake Him, He will reject you forever. Consider now, for the Lord has chosen you to build a house as the sanctuary. Be strong and do the work."
—1 Chronicles 28:9-10

What do you think of when you hear the word conscience? An ethereal sense of right and wrong? Or maybe Disney's Jiminy Cricket from *Pinocchio*—a smartly dressed insect who tells the wooden boy to "give a little whistle" when he needs moral guidance?

The word conscience comes from the Latin verb *conscire* [com (with) + scire (to know)] meaning "with knowing" or "knowing together." What "knowing" should guide our lives and work as artists?

King David's words in 1 Chronicles 28-29 give us three areas of "knowing" to consider.

WE ARE TO KNOW THE LORD

Between the sixth and tenth century BCE, King David commissioned his son Solomon to build the Jerusalem Temple. This architectural marvel represented the Lord's Presence with Israel—but it would mean nothing if Solomon did not put knowing the Lord as his first priority. Likewise, artists who follow Jesus are first called into relationship, then into practice. Just as painters study the Masters, we sit at the feet of our Master to learn from Him, know His heart, and walk in His ways. This "knowing" allows us to discern whether our art and the Lord's heart are aligned—and lovingly nudges us if we veer into pride, self-glory, or distraction.

WE ARE TO KNOW OUR CRAFT

David then passes Solomon the blueprints to the temple—a labour of "all my might" and "my affection."[28] Whether you are an amateur (one who loves) or a professional, our love for our craft is often reflected in our craft. The musician experiments with new chord shapes, the poet with prosody, the painter with colour. The better we know our tools, the better we can express the soul of the art. Of course, we can always see the flaws in our work. Conscience allows us to discern whether a flaw undermines the art, or adds unexpected depth. In the book *The Boy, the Mole, the Fox, and the Horse* by Charlie Mackesy, an illustration is covered with watercolour splotches as Mackesy's dog had walked

---

[28] 1 Chronicles 29:2-3

across the wet page. Mackesy recognised that this imperfection only deepened the page's message: "The greatest illusion... is that life should be perfect."[29]

WE ARE TO KNOW OUR COMMUNITY

The design of the Jewish temple reflected the cultural identity and reality of the Jewish people, while also lifting their imagination to the heavenly realms. The Lord has placed each of us in the context of community. We were born in a particular time, location, language, and culture. As listeners and observers, we then learn how to speak to our people. The American singer-songwriter Johnny Cash put it this way: "You've got a song you're singing from your gut, you want that audience to feel it in their gut. And you've got to make them think that you're one of them sitting out there with them too. They've got to be able to relate to what you're doing." Not everyone may understand art, but we shouldn't let carelessness or self-absorption be the reason.

David's final encouragement is this: be strong and do the work. We are at no shortage of voices that place their expectations on our lives and art. Strength is required to discern artistic vision, to dutifully pursue it, and to beautifully complete it. So let our artist's conscience be our guide—the still small voice shaped by Creator, community, and craft—so we can become co-laborers with the divine.

---

[29] Charlie Mackesy, *The Boy, the Mole, the Fox, and the Horse*, 2019, Collins, p.69

APPLICATION

Using the guidance of the *Examen*,[30] ask the Holy Spirit to guide you as you look back over your journey of artistry. Offer gratitude for those people and experiences that have shaped these areas of knowing. Do you feel a loving nudge to push deeper in any area? Ask the Holy Spirit to show you how you might pursue this more, not out of guilt, but out of love. Finally, look forward to the opportunity to go, as C.S. Lewis put it, "further up, and further in."[31]

PRAYER

O Whisper of Wisdom—whose still small voice speaks beyond the earthquake, fire, and wind, and calls us by name—come, speak to us again through the turbulence of our hearts and minds in our pursuit of truth and beauty. Give us courage of conviction and conscience—transforming our minds to be aligned with You, our hearts with love for those we serve—and diligence to steward well our talents and skills in this Kingdom of our Lord Jesus Christ, who lives and reigns with You and the Holy Spirit, one God, now and forever. Amen.

---

[30] For an introduction to the Examen, please see www.jesuits.org/spirituality/the-ignatian-examen/

[31] C.S. Lewis, *The Last Battle*, 1956, Macmillan, pp.195-197

Reflective & Artistic Practices

BY PETER ASSAD

"The real work of the artist is a way of being in the world."
—Rick Rubin[32]

PART 1: ARTIST'S EXAMEN

An optional journaling practice to close this five-chapter journey with prayerful reflection.

Prelude: Entering Sacred Space
Find a quiet place where you can sit comfortably and focus your thoughts. Dim the lights. Draw the curtains. Light a candle, if it helps. Take a few moments to breathe deeply, allowing your body and mind to find stillness.

---

[32] Rick Rubin, *The Creative Act: A Way of Being*, 2023, PenguinPress, p.34

Prayer to begin:

God of beauty and calling, as I reflect on the road that's brought me here, help me see where You've been walking beside me—guiding, shaping, and gently nudging me forward.

For reflection:

1. Gratitude: Where have I seen God's hand in my creative gift recently? What brings me joy?

2. Story: When do I feel most alive—or most vulnerable—as an artist? What may that be telling me?

3. Integration: In what ways is the creative process molding my heart to look more like Jesus?

4. Dialogue: What do I want to say to God, and what might He be saying back?

5. Hope: What kind of artist do I sense God is shaping me to become?

Closing:

The Spirit of the Lord is upon you, because He has anointed you to proclaim good news to the poor... to set the captives free... to proclaim the year of the Lord's favor.[33] Your art is an offering of worship, a channel of healing, and a sacred portal into the beauty of Christ in all the world. May you rest in the confidence of the calling He has placed on your life.

---

[33] Adapted from Luke 4:18-19

PART 2: ARTISTIC PRACTICE

Choose one of the following creative responses. Let it be simple. This is not about skill—it's about showing up with honesty and curiosity.

Option 1: Draw Your Artist's Compass
Sketch a symbol, image, or simple diagram that represents your artistic "true north." What values or themes guide you as an artist in Christ? No need for detail—let it be instinctual.

Option 2: Letter to Your Future Artist Self
Write a short letter to yourself five years from now. Begin with: "I hope you still..." or "Remember when..." What do you hope to still believe, practice, or wrestle with in your creative life? To go a step further, mail it to yourself and keep it sealed away to read in five years.

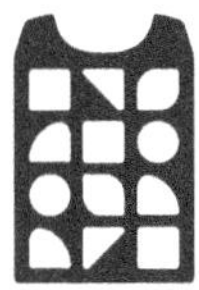

PART THREE:
WALKING WITH OUR CRAFT

"The Church's approach to an intelligent carpenter is usually confined to exhorting him not to be drunk and disorderly in his leisure hours, and to come to church on Sundays. What the Church should be telling him is this: that the very first demand that his religion makes upon him is that he should make good tables. Church by all means, and decent forms of amusement, certainly—but what use is all that if in the very center of his life and occupation he is insulting God with bad carpentry? No crooked table legs or ill-fitting drawers ever, I dare swear, came out of the carpenter's shop at Nazareth. Nor, if they did, could anyone believe that they were made by the same hand that made heaven and earth."

—Dorothy Day[34]

---

34 Dorothy Day, *Letters to a Diminished Church*, 2004, Thomas Nelson, p.132

11. Sowing and Sabbath

BY CAMERON MILLER

"The bow cannot be always bent without fear of breaking. Repose is as needful to the mind as sleep to the body... Rest time is not waste time. It is economy to gather fresh strength."
—*Charles Spurgeon*[35]

Read: Leviticus 25:1-7

I am a writer. There's nothing that brings me more joy than having written something excellent. And there's nothing that brings me more despair than trying to write something excellent. Some days I get a wonderful idea in my head, but as soon as I sit down that crystal-clear picture turns milky and fades. Other days I make myself write, but every word on the page is one I know I'm going to end up

---

[35] Charles Spurgeon, *Lectures to My Students*, 1875, Passmore and Alabaster, p.174

deleting tomorrow. And still other days, I want to create but have no ideas worth writing. I need a way to cultivate my craft so that these situations don't hold me back as often. And as I talk with God and meditate on Scripture, I've started to recognize a pattern that I think might be crucial in getting there.

I'm taking inspiration from the Lord's commands about working and resting in Leviticus 25. The Israelites work six days and rest on the seventh. For six years straight they do hard, back-breaking labor to force the ground to produce as much bounty as it possibly can, and in the seventh year they let it lie fallow and grow what it will, allowing the soil to replenish its nutrients and recover. This is the pattern the Lord God has built into the fabric of the universe, and I'm starting to think it applies to art as well.

IF YOU WANT TO REAP, YOU NEED TO SOW

When I'm stuck in my writing, often the only way out is through. It's discouraging to struggle for two hours and get only a pair of measly sentences that I'll be rewriting tomorrow—but it's part of the process. When I come back after a period of not writing regularly it's hard at first, but eventually writing begins to trickle and then flow freely. With dedication and diligence, eventually it comes. If you want to be the kind of person who regularly creates art, you can't wait for inspiration. You have to sit down and practice being the person you want to be.

SABBATH IS ESSENTIAL

As important as dedication and perseverance are, rest is also essential —a cessation of striving. God commanded the Israelites to let the land rest every seven years. They did not spend the seventh year fasting; they were free to pick anything the land produced on its own. But they couldn't force it to produce things it no longer had the capacity to bear. And the plants most likely to thrive in that depleted soil were the ones God designed to put back what had been taken away by the years of harsh farming.

It's crucial for us as artists to periodically step back and let our minds relax—stop forcing ourselves to produce. If you're finding art stressful, if you've fallen into a rut, if the process is draining you dry, you might just be ready for a season of rest. In this time you stop worrying about what you think other people want you to produce, you stop pushing yourself to create far after your heart has told you it's had enough, and you let whatever happens happen. If no ideas spring up, you don't create art. If something sounds fun, you do it as a hobby. You doodle, you write fanfic, or you dabble. You try what seems interesting rather than the things you know you can succeed at. Or you focus on other parts of life and set down the art supplies for a while.

RHYTHMS OF REST

Now, these ideas may seem to run counter to each other, but the harmony is found in rhythms of rest. Write for 60 minutes and get up and stretch for ten. Work on your painting for six days and take a day off to step back and give your mind a break. And if you've spent the last six years recording songs and churning out albums but are finding that everything you make is sounding the same, maybe it's time to step back from songwriting and try something new, just to get out of the rut.

One of the biggest confrontations Jesus had with the Pharisees was over the Sabbath. They claimed it was a time for man to strive and struggle not to do anything that could be considered work. Jesus claimed it was a time for rest. And then He fulfilled the law so we are no longer under its burden. Rhythms of rest are not a legal burden placed on the shoulders of our craft; they are how God has ordered the universe, His plan for our creative good.

APPLICATION

Take a page in your journal or a sheet of paper and divide it into "fields"—simple straight lines are fine, or you might want to add trees, a river, or other landscape features. Label individual fields with a specific aspect of your creativity e.g. song writing, painting, embroidery, woodworking. If you need to add more fields, do—and don't worry if some fields are left blank! Sit before God with this visual representation of your artistic cultivation and talk with Him about where you need to sow, where you need to tend, which fields are ready for harvest, and which need to lie fallow for a season.

PRAYER

Lord, thank You for creating me in Your image—a God who works and who rests. Help me learn the holy rhythm of diligence and restoration. When I'm discouraged by lack of progress, remind me that every seed sown matters. And when I'm worn thin by striving, teach me to stop and simply be. Guide my hands and my heart to create in step with Your Spirit. Amen.

12. Birthing Universes

BY PETER ASSAD

"My immediate result was not to consult any human being... but I went into Arabia."
—*Galatians 1:16-17*

I'll admit, there are times when I get frustrated with my own creative process. You know those moments when an idea is swirling around in your head, and you're desperate to get it out—yet it feels like you're just staring at a blank page, unsure of how to bring it to life? The struggle is real. I often find myself brooding in these times—easily irritable, frustrated—caught between the vision of what could be and the reality of what isn't yet. But what if brooding isn't the enemy of creativity? What if it's the very space where God births universes?

In Genesis 1:2, we read that the Spirit of God "hovered" over the waters at the very beginning of time. That word "hovered," or *rāḥap* in Hebrew, is the same word we use for brooding. Before creation took shape, before anything was visible or tangible, the Spirit was at work—quietly moving, waiting, and preparing. That word *rāḥap* shows up in just two other places in all the Bible. First, in Deuteronomy 32:11, where an eagle broods over her young, gently stirring the nest to prepare them for flight, and in Jeremiah 23:9, where the prophet is brooding, struggling with the weight of God's message.

As artists, we know that "brooding" all too well. When an idea takes root, it often starts in a quiet, messy place. It's the period where nothing is visible—nothing feels ready. But it's this place of "brooding" where creativity is incubated. Instead of rushing it, what if we embraced that process, trusting God is at work in the hidden spaces as He was in the beginning? This is exactly what we see when the Apostle Paul received his radical call to preach to the Gentiles. After his dramatic conversion, he didn't rush to the apostles or align himself with established voices for advice or validation. Instead, he withdrew to the deserts of Arabia—a season of solitude and formation where God Himself shaped his calling. Hidden away in that wilderness, his purpose was incubated. And when the time was right, God sent him out to proclaim the gospel to the world.

As the Spirit hovered over creation, as an eagle broods over her nest, as a prophet bears the weight of God's words for his people— what new thing is God birthing within our brooding?

There are times I lose sight of this in my own brooding, which usually results in a moody, temperamental, insufferable artist to be around. But when I lift my eyes to recognize these periods as the tension of birthing something new, something shifts inside me. After all, wasn't it Christ who sweat great drops of blood in Gethsemane, pleading "let this cup pass from me"?[36] Wasn't it Christ who cried aloud, "My God, my God, why have You forsaken me"[37] as He bore the weight of the world on the cross? And wasn't it Christ who, after enduring that process, was able to declare, "It is finished"[38]—ushering in the new creation?

Perhaps, in a way, all creative brooding is a manifestation of the new thing the Spirit of God is bringing into the world... through us.

APPLICATION

- ❖ Are you in a season where it feels like nothing is coming together creatively? Maybe God is calling you to embrace that space of brooding. Don't rush through the waiting. Let God nurture what is forming inside you. Just like a seed needs time to grow before it's visible, your creative work is likely growing in unseen ways. Trust that He is preparing you to be a conduit for something out of this world.

- ❖ Where do you feel the tension between what you know is inside of you and the frustration of not being able to express it yet? What would change in your attitude if you reframed that tension as simply the Spirit of God brooding over your creativity? Just as He hovered over creation, He is patiently waiting for the right moment for your work to emerge. Instead of trying to force it, take a step back to allow His process to unfold.

---

[36] Matthew 26:39 (KJV)

[37] Matthew 27:46

[38] John 19:30

God, I invite You into my creative process today. I admit that there are times when I grow frustrated, feel stuck, and wonder if anything is truly happening. Help me to trust You in these moments—the quiet, hidden spaces where You are incubating something new. Give me patience in the waiting and faith that You are at work, even when I can't see it. Let my creativity flow from Your Spirit, and may it reflect the beauty of new creation. Amen.

13. Diligence as an Offering

by Cameron Miller

"Perseverance does not mean 'perfection.' It means that we keep going. We do not quit when we find that we are not yet mature and there is a long journey still before us."

—Eugene Peterson[39]

As artists, we all enjoy the times when inspiration gushes from the fountain, when everything flows smoothly and we love what we're doing. In those times it's easy to create art. But other times we go to the well, we pump the handle until our arm aches, and all we get is a few drops in an empty bucket. It's heartbreaking. What do we do?

We looked in "Chapter 11: Sowing and Sabbath" at the importance of rhythms of rest in our creativity—like a farmer letting the land rest and be replenished so that a more bountiful crop may

---

39 Eugene Peterson, *A Long Obedience in the Same Direction*, 1980, IVP, p.131

come next season. But sometimes you rest, and the land is restored, yet no crops grow. And in such a case you do what every farmer knows must be done: you go out and you plant and plow and water and put in ten times the effort even if you only get a tenth of what you normally would.

This may seem pointless. If an artist's job is to create art, and all that work produces a scant, starved crop, doesn't that just mean failure as an artist? Our culture values us by what we produce, but God looks at the heart. Does He not see your struggles? Does He not count your tears as you cry them? Certainly He is glorified by the fruit of your labor, but is He not glorified more when you work to praise Him though your flesh fails and your earthly mind tells you it's accomplishing nothing? We artists cannot always achieve the results we strive for, but we can choose the effort we offer to God. It is this choice that honors God most, not the results.

Furthermore, there is value in practice. A martial artist will practice his forms day after day even when no enemy is present so that, when the battle comes, he is ready to strike. An athlete will train all year for an event that only lasts seconds so that, when the challenge arrives, she can win the prize. So, we must be diligent in practicing our art. A lack of inspiration makes this trying, but it also offers us a chance to hone our fundamentals and refine our technique. All artists receive inspiration. Those who practice faithfully will find their bodies and minds prepared, ready to make full use of the inspiration they receive. Improvisational artists know this best. How do they get up on stage and spontaneously create art, working without a plan or pattern to copy? That freedom comes from years of diligent repetition where the basic movements of their art become so ingrained that they can effortlessly perform them as the inspiration flows through them.

In all this, I picture Elijah on Mount Carmel.[40] He has built an altar, set the wood, prepared the sacrifice, and gathered the people to see what his God can do. All that is left is for God to send the fire. Elijah has done all he can to make things ready for what God has in store next. Likewise, our dedication in preparing is a sacrificial offering that is difficult and painful to make. And yet this sole act of making-ready honors God. Our diligence in rehearsing prepares us as a living sacrifice, ready to be used according to God's purposes. There may be times when we are waiting for God to send the fire, and we wait, and wait... But when the fire comes, let the world beware, because nothing will stop or hinder it.

If you are in the doldrums creatively, if nothing is happening and all efforts seem wasted, do not be discouraged. Instead, prepare yourself for what God is doing next. Because it is coming. You will create wondrous things again.

If you're wondering how you'll ever live up to what God has planned, know that it was never resting on you to begin with. When God sets out to accomplish His purposes, no force in heaven or earth will stop Him. He loves you and wants to give you the opportunity to take part in what He's doing.

So, practice! Condition your mind to imagine and your hands to create. Don't give up, because God wastes nothing that is entrusted to Him. As you are making yourself ready, He is getting excited about what He is going to place in your waiting hands.

---

40 1 Kings 18

APPLICATION

Use words, images, music, or movement to describe either a time in your life when practicing had a significant impact on your craft, or another artist you know who embodies this approach to creativity. As you do, reflect on how God is inviting you to make an offering of diligence to Him in whatever creative season you find yourself in.

PRAYER

Lord, when inspiration fades and all my efforts feel empty and dry, remind me that what honors You isn't perfection but perseverance. Make me faithful as You are faithful, trusting that You are at work even in the waiting. Like Elijah, may I prepare the altar with diligence, holding out hope for the fire that will come in Your time. Amen.

14. The Slipstream of Stewardship

by Cath Butler

"And stewardship is about taking care of what is most valuable and accomplishing together what all of us most want to get done."
—Tod Bolsinger[41]

Read: Matthew 25:14-30

From the creation mandate to co-reigning in the new creation, the biblical idea of human stewardship is full of flourishing—for the physical resources God has put at our disposal, our own gifts, and even churches or ministries and the people that are part of them. We

---

[41] Tod Bolsinger, *Tempered Resilience: How Leaders Are Formed in the Crucible of Change,* 2020, IVP, p.4

are, Paul says, "servants of Christ and stewards of the mysteries of God."[42] How incredible to think that, as we take care of all that has been entrusted to us, we get to steward the mysteries of God—the revelation of who He is and what He's done, His story in our lives and beyond, the glimpses of His beauty, goodness, and truth that we barely have words for and turn to our creativity to express.

Stewardship is also intertwined with an invitation to faithfulness. In the parable of the talents, Jesus tells the story of a man of means preparing for a period of absence by entrusting his finances to his servants. Appointing them his business representatives, he trusts them to know him well enough to choose what would please him... and it turns out this means investing what he has given.

Investment—now, as then—is characterised by using what we have in a well-judged way in the hope of an increased return. It's all too easy to fixate on the return, but what seems more important to Jesus in this story is the courage and discernment required to risk what we have been given wisely. This, not the specific amount achieved, is what received the master's commendation of faithfulness, and it flowed from a fearless relationship with him. There's such freedom for us in this: freedom to focus on faithfully exercising courage and discernment in how we use and invest in our creativity, for One we serve without fear, unhindered by anxiety about the return. What might that look like—to create freely, courageously, and discerningly, from a place of fearless and trusting relationship with God, leaving the results in His hands?

Those results are God's anyway: what we start with is His, and whatever more is made goes back to Him. Our reward isn't the return

---

[42] 1 Corinthians 4:1

—that goes to God. Our reward is greater responsibility! It makes me wonder how God wants to surprise us as we invest our creativity for Him, how He might want to expand our expectations: from hoping our creativity might earn us the reward of personal success, to seeing and stepping further into the privileged stewardship He wants to offer us. Whilst we, as faithful stewards, are to invest for increase for our Master, He is the one who gives increased influence. It can be hard not to run ahead of Him in this—pursuing bigger platforms, pouting when our art doesn't reach a wider audience—but our part is to be trustworthy with the opportunities He gives us, however big or small, allowing Him to choose when He gives us wider influence.

What I love about this parable is the space Jesus creates for me between the extremes of fearfully hiding my creativity and grasping at its success for personal gain. Like a cyclist just ahead, Jesus pedals towards the Kingdom and pulls me into the slipstream of stewardship where—one foot on discerning courage, one foot on faithfulness—I can move forward with Him and in His purposes. When I veer towards creative abdication, struggling to share my art because I've already decided it's worthless, He reminds me to push on using what He's given me courageously and well. When I swerve into arrogant fantasies about my songs being sung by the masses, He reminds me to faithfully press into His Kingdom in whatever ways He has already opened to me. There is such grace here.

So, let's pursue confidence in relationship with our Creator, and the faithful exercise of courage and discernment in our creativity. As artists, let's take well-judged risks in how we invest our creativity, placing it where it can grow, all so that we have something to offer back to the One who gave it all. It's all from Him, it's all for Him, and if we centre our creative practice on Him, we may well find ourselves surprised at what He has waiting for us.

APPLICATION

- ❖ Perhaps you already know what it is like to risk your time, heart, skills, money, and artwork in hope of creative return. Or maybe in this moment you sense Jesus' invitation to dig your creativity out of the place you've hidden it and dare to place it where it can grow. Either way, how is He inviting you further into courageous and discerning risk in your creativity?
- ❖ Take a moment to be still and allow the Holy Spirit to search your heart about the "return" you hope for from your creativity: honestly, honestly, is it for you or for Him?
- ❖ How does it feel to know that God trusts you to know Him well enough to choose what would please Him? Journal about what this stirs in you, and about how your perception of and relationship with God impact your creative praxis.

PRAYER

Holy Spirit, thank You for the creative gifts You have entrusted to me. Please fill me with all the courage, discernment, and humility I need to faithfully steward my creativity for Your purposes... and let me know the joy of pursuing Kingdom growth with You.

15. You Are Loosed!

by Kathryn Kircher

"It is for freedom that Christ has set us free. Stand firm, then, and do not let yourselves be burdened again by a yoke of slavery."
—Galatians 5:1

Read: Luke 13:10-17

Eighteen years! Eighteen long, brutal years. You can't imagine the perpetual pain and torment I've endured. I've been doubled over with the weight of it, unable to stand up straight this entire time. I couldn't lift my head. I saw nothing but the feet of the people around me. It was impossible to raise myself up.

But Jesus did it for me—He raised me up with a touch of His hand on my shoulder and four little words: "Woman, you are loosed!"

Here I am, straight and tall! I'd given up hope that I'd ever be able to stand erect again. But I'm free! Free of pain. Free of the bondage I've endured for 18 years. The weight of it all has consumed me for almost two decades. The "healers" and their so-called treatments that never cured me. The limitations of being bent in two. The inner torment and turmoil. The excruciating pain itself. It all absorbed every bit of my strength, my time, and my attention.

Now what? I hardly know what to do with myself! What new doors are open to me? What am I going to do with all that energy and focus I've regained? The possibilities are mind-boggling. The "can'ts" have been replaced with "cans"!

Selah

This woman's health—and the spirit of darkness that caused it—controlled her life for 18 years. The limitations she faced, bent over double and unable to lift her head, would impact every aspect of her life, even if she lived in our day and culture. How much worse would her confinement have been 2,000 years ago with social taboos, limited healthcare, and no access to resources like physical and occupational therapy, medications, or modern medical equipment? This woman experienced a release beyond imagination when Jesus said, "You are loosed!" Let's allow that to ignite a fire of hope in our hearts!

We've all had areas where Jesus has untied us and set us free like He did for this woman—although maybe not quite so dramatic. For me, liberation has been a gradual, subtle process. As I've become more firmly grounded in my identity as a treasured child of God, holy and pleasing to Him, I've slowly but surely found myself freer to express myself as a writer and to explore new genres. I've even ventured into other artforms, experimenting with watercolor and singing with a local Bach ensemble. Knowing who I am in Christ—and realizing that I'm supposed to be unique—has loosed the destructive grip of comparison and helped me begin to unravel the long-term habit of striving to fit in and be like everyone else. I may not have been bent over in two like the woman whose story is chronicled here, but I was hindered—and sometimes even crippled—by fear of what others might think of me.

For me, liberation has come through knowing how dearly I am loved and how priceless I am in God's eyes—by realizing that the Trinity is enamored with me and delights in the characteristics that make me unique. How about you? What does, "You are loosed!" look like in your life?

APPLICATION

If Jesus can liberate this woman who faced such unimaginable barriers to freedom, what might He do in the areas where we are being held back—especially in our creativity? Let's take some time to ponder:

- ❖ What are some of the specific ways God has loosed you? How has that impacted your creativity? What new possibilities or works of art have emerged in the wake of His freeing work?

- ❖ How have limitations impacted your creativity—both positively and negatively? What workarounds have you discovered that have equipped you to continue to create, even in the face of hindrances or limitations?

- ❖ Where are some of the places in your life where you'd like to see the Trinity bring more freedom? Imagine what your life—including your creativity—might look like without these confines that hold you back.

PRAYER

Lord of Liberty, thank You for the ways You have loosed me and set me free, especially ____________. Thank You for creative workarounds. Thank You for the moments of both sudden liberation and gradually emerging release. Thank You for the freedom that is still to come, especially ____________. You're my Deliverer, my Savior, my Liberator, my Emancipator! I love You and honor You. Amen.

Reflective & Artistic Practices

BY MICHAEL STALCUP

PART 1: DEVELOP A CREATIVE RULE OF LIFE

A Rule of Life is a schedule of regular rhythms and practices that helps us to flourish. While the word "rule" may sound restrictive, the goal of a Rule of Life is freedom to steward our lives and gifts effectively. For example, the discipline of a weekly Sabbath day helps to free a person from a life of overwork and unhealthy self-reliance. Similarly, the discipline of painting for 30 minutes a week helps to free an artist to be able to paint things they could never otherwise paint.

Sketch out a Creative Rule of Life for yourself and your craft. Start out by splitting a page into sections for each of the following frequencies: daily, weekly, monthly, quarterly, annually. Feel free to write down in these sections any current practices you want to be intentional about continuing.

Then add one new rhythm (or two, at most) that you want to focus on incorporating over the next few weeks. To decide what rhythm(s) would be helpful, ask yourself these questions:

- ❖ What qualities or skills do I want to develop as an artist?
- ❖ What is preventing me?

❖ What practice would help me grow into the artist I want to become?

Keep your rhythms achievable. It is better to write for 30 minutes a week and build a solid habit than to ambitiously attempt 30 minutes a day and give up after a week.

Set a date (perhaps a month from now) to revisit your Creative Rule of Life. Don't feel guilty about any goals you have not kept. Rather, observe why you did not keep those goals and revise your Rule of Life accordingly. The Creative Rule of Life is a living document that should change to fit different seasons of life. The point is to remain intentional about who you are becoming. Enjoy it!

PART 2: COME BEFORE GOD THROUGH ART-AS-PRAYER

Although there are times we slip into fearfully hiding our creativity from God, Scripture calls us to "approach the throne of grace with confidence."[43] There, we focus not on our own failures and successes, but on finding our identity in the finished work of Jesus—freeing us to fulfill God's calling on our lives with peace and courage.

In Psalm 32, King David gives powerful voice to these contrasting themes of hiding from God and coming before God. "When I kept silent, my bones wasted away through my groaning all day long," he writes (v.3). Yet when David stopped hiding and came before God in his brokenness, he found God to be a true and safe "hiding place" where he was embraced and restored with "songs of deliverance" (v.7). David's poem begins with lonely struggle but ends with rejoicing in God's healing.

---

[43] Hebrews 4:16

Set aside 30 minutes to create a work of art in any artistic medium (poetry, painting, composing, dancing etc.) that reflects these contrasting themes of hiding and coming before God. Let the creation of this art be a form of prayer. First, creatively express an element of brokenness, fear, or sin you experience as an artist, letting your creative act bring this struggle into the loving Presence of God. Second, spend a few moments in prayer listening to God, then creatively express your sense of God's response—of forgiveness, restoration, truth, love, or whatever else you sense God speaking to you through prayer or Scripture. Whether you create two separate art pieces or one work of art that incorporates both themes, may your art serve as a reminder to you and others that "the Lord's unfailing love surrounds the one who trusts in Him" (v.10).

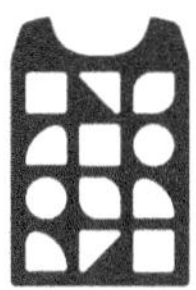

PART FOUR:
WALKING WITH THE KINGDOM

"They are not, themselves, building the cathedral, but they are building for the cathedral, and when the cathedral is complete their work will be enhanced, ennobled, will mean much more than it could have meant as they were chiseling it and shaping it down in the stonemasons' yard."
—*N.T. Wright*[44]

44 N.T. Wright, *Surprised by Hope: Rethinking Heaven, the Resurrection, and the Mission of the Church*, 2008, SPCK, pp.209-210

16. The Thin Places of Our Lives

BY SHARON JONES

"Therefore, brothers and sisters, since we have confidence to enter the Most Holy Place by the blood of Jesus, by a new and living way opened for us through the curtain, that is, His body... Let us hold unswervingly to the hope we profess, for He who promised is faithful."
—Hebrews 10:19-23

In my Irish imagination, thin places are wild and wind-swept: far-flung fields of standing-stones shrouded in mist, or lonely stretches of rugged Atlantic coastline. As Joel Busby writes, "Celtic believers thought of thin places as physical, geographic locations where the barrier between heaven and earth is porous because the Lord, in His kindness, met a person there."[45] Dramatic land and seascapes are certainly awe inspiring, but encounters with God can be closer to home. God met Joel on a little hospital bench when his wife was gravely ill. Wherever God meets us, He lifts our eyes to the day when the dwelling place of God will always be with man, and every place will be thin.

According to Malcolm Guite, "It is the special gift of the imaginative arts... to help us see how any place might suddenly become the very gate of heaven."[46] Art is indeed a gift, for we know that apart from God's kindness none of us could create anything. As Saint John explains, "Through Him all things were made; without Him nothing was made that has been made" (John 1:3). Lewis Hyde, in his book *The Gift,* depicts the creative process itself as a "gifted state." It's a question of grace: the artist is gifted with ideas, but also with the ability to transform those ideas into art. Hyde suggests that "in those moments when we are gifted, the work falls together graciously."[47] Or, as one of my friends put it, when she paints prayerfully and her work is progressing, she experiences God's good pleasure.

Through our physical senses in art, God has gifted us with the possibility of not only experiencing His love, but communicating it to others. In my life, music is a powerful example of this. And gardens help me picture it too, as places of colour and fragrance, texture and beauty. They are marked by intricate design, the interplay of light and shade, and the nourishment and restoration of water. Most of all,

---

[45] www.thegospelcoalition.org/article/gifts-thin-place/

[46] Malcolm Guite, *Lifting the Veil: Imagination and the Kingdom of God*, 2022, Canterbury Press, p. 26

[47] Lewis Hyde, *The Gift: How the Creative Spirit Transforms the World*, 2012, Canongate, p. 195

they are places of resurrection. Perhaps that's why Scripture is book-ended with gardens, why the imagery of trees and gardens graced the design of the Temple and the Tabernacle, and why gardens are writ so large in the life and teaching of Jesus. He even called God His Father "the Gardener!"[48]

Chapters 1-3 of the book of Genesis remind us that God did indeed plant a garden, at the beginning of time. He walked in the garden in the cool of the day, and He appointed Adam and Eve to look after it. In the centuries afterwards, leading up to the birth of Jesus, God often revealed Himself not in some mystical state, but in a physical way. He appeared to Moses in the flames of a burning bush.[49] He wrestled with Jacob at Peniel.[50] He spoke to Elijah in a still small voice.[51] And as David Taylor writes, for Tabernacle worship, God "commissions Moses to create a specific incense and then trademarks it."[52] God cares about what things look like, how they sound and taste, how they feel, and even how they smell! For artists, there is something enormously affirming about all this, because creative work is sensory, and every detail matters to God.

In the Incarnation, God acknowledges the role our human physical senses play in encountering Him. When Mary and Joseph gazed upon the child Jesus, the veil of heaven was swept aside, for God Himself had come to find us. Jesus is the ultimate thin place, because in Jesus heaven and earth have come together. And when Jesus died the curtain in the Temple was torn in two, opening up for

---

[48] John 15:1

[49] Exodus 3

[50] Genesis 32:22-32

[51] 1 Kings 19:11-13

[52] W. David O. Taylor, *A Body of Praise: Understanding the Role of Our Physical Bodies in Worship*, 2023, Baker Books, p. 83

us a new and living way. In this new and living way, the Holy Spirit dwells within us. Our bodies become temples so that our lives—as individuals and in community—can become thin places. It's amazing to think that people might see something of Christ in each of our lives, and also in our creating. Christ in us—this is the hope of glory![53]

God loves to draw near to us; He loves thin places. As artists, we can encounter Him not only in wild and windswept places but right where we are: at our easels and workbenches, our writing desks and galleries, our kitchens and our gardens. For when we seek Him, God meets us in our making; He satisfies our artistic calling. But more than that, He allows our lives and our art to bless others, inviting them into thin places too. Let us continue to offer our bodies as a living sacrifice to God, so that each ordinary day of our living and making might become a thin place—a place for the Lord to draw near, just where we are, to make His kindness known.

APPLICATION

- ❖ Reflect on temples and trees in Scripture, using this resource from The Bible Project: https://bibleproject.com/classroom/ephesians/sessions/21. Consider drawing or describing the kind of temple or tree you would like your creativity to become.
- ❖ Listen prayerfully to the song "Holy Spirit Living Breath of God" (https://youtu.be/kDYjn-YdnD4) from Ireland by Keith and Kristyn Getty. Journal about what it stirs in you.

---

[53] Colossians 1:27

PRAYER

Holy Lord, thank You for drawing near to us in Jesus; thank You for opening up a new and living way through Him. Creator God, thank You for the gift of our senses, and for the gift of art. Please use the gifts that You have given us to point others to Christ and to bring You glory. Gracious Lord, may the ordinary days of my living and all my creative work be like a temple or a beautiful garden—a thin place where You can draw near to us in Your kindness. Living Lord, through Your Holy Spirit, breathe life into all of my making; draw me—and all of us—closer, in all things, to You.

17. Imago Dei

BY GRACE ASSAD

"Those who were able to forgive their former enemies were able also to return to the outside world and rebuild their lives, no matter what the physical scars. Those who nursed their bitterness remained invalids. It was as simple and as horrible as that."
—*Corrie Ten Boom*

If we are made in the image of God—whether collectively or individually—then every human interaction I have can teach me something new about Him. Some aspect of His remarkable, multi-faceted character is brought into sharper focus having seen it in another.

You can see it in those considered "lowly." As a NICU nurse, I've cared for some of the most medically-complex patients. By American standards of success and independence, a neurologically devastated ventilator-dependent 17-month-old with a tracheostomy and gastrostomy tube who cannot yet sit upright might not be seen as "thriving." But in God's upside-down Kingdom, this child is a radiant image-bearer. Her smile reflects His joy. Her laughter at a silly YouTube song, or delight in a light-up toy, reveals something of His delight in simple things. She isn't anxious about her needs being met—she trusts implicitly that she will be cared for. And within God's family, that trust is honored. Her life holds immeasurable value not because of her ability, but because of His image in her.

Pretty soon I realize that I am the one in need. I am anxious about tomorrow. I am hurrying past opportunities to delight in the world around me, distracted by "more important" things. She is my teacher, and her life speaks volumes if only I have eyes to see.

God's image also resides in those who have wounded us deeply. Jesus calls us to love our enemies—a command that cuts against every natural instinct. How can we possibly see God's face in someone who has caused us harm?

Corrie Ten Boom wrestled with this very question. Years after surviving the horrors of Ravensbrück concentration camp, where she was paraded naked in front of guards and watched her sister suffer and die, Corrie encountered one of those guards. After she had preached a message of forgiveness in a Swedish church, the man, now a believer, approached her—hand extended, seeking her forgiveness.

She was faced with a terrible question: could she see God's image in his face—even through the humiliation, suffering, and terror of her history with this man?

It echoes the biblical moment when Ananias was called to lay hands on Saul—a man notorious for persecuting Christians. Ananias objected: "Lord, I have heard many reports about this man..." (Acts 9:13). But God sent him anyway. And Ananias obeyed. He laid his hands on Saul and said, "Brother Saul" (Acts 9:17). With those words, scales fell from Saul's eyes, and he was transformed.

Corrie writes of that holy moment with her former abuser: "For a long moment we grasped each other's hands, the former guard and the former prisoner. I had never known God's love so intensely as I did then."

God's intense love. His intense love that drove Him to take on our lowly, burdensome skin and tabernacle among us. His intense love that fueled every human interaction He had—at parties, in the marketplace, on mountainsides, on boats, at wells, and in the middle of mobs ready to throw stones. His intense love that drew Him to the unloved, discarded, and hated in His society. His intense love that drove Him to hang on a cross for enemies who mocked Him. His wounds healed us, so that "we might die to sin and live for righteousness."[54] When I hold on to bitterness, it poisons me—often far more than it ever affects the one who hurt me. Corrie saw this clearly in the lives of fellow survivors: those who embraced forgiveness found the strength to rebuild, while those who clung to resentment remained trapped in their pain. I have a choice. I can look into the faces of those who oppose me and, by faith in the One wounded on my behalf, recognize the image of God. And in doing so, I can forgive.

In the lowly our world would ignore, and in enemies the world shouts for us to hate, we are called to see the face of God—and He is beautiful.

APPLICATION

As artists, we are called to help the world see the unseen—to bring light into places of darkness, rejection, and pain. Our creativity can

---

54 1 Peter 2:24

become a holy protest against bitterness and a sacred witness to God's intense love.

Allow these reflection questions to stir your creative practice:

- ❖ What might it look like to engage creatively with the story of someone you are tempted to consider "lowly"?
- ❖ Who do you need to forgive? How can you begin to see them through God's eyes?
- ❖ How might your art help dismantle enemy-making and rebuild bridges of compassion?
- ❖ Create a piece (song, painting, poem etc.) that imagines seeing the face of God in someone you've struggled to understand or accept.

PRAYER

Lord, make me an instrument of Your peace:
where there is hatred, let me sow love;
where there is injury, pardon;
where there is doubt, faith;
where there is despair, hope;
where there is darkness, light;
and where there is sadness, joy.

Help me see Your image in those I'd rather not see,
and recognize Your face in surprising places.
Heal the wounds that others have left in me,
until my wounds heal others.
Teach me to love not only the lovely,
but also those I fear, resent, or misunderstand—
that my art would be an echo of Your grace,

a mirror of Your mercy—
because Your love is intense,
and You are in them, too.
Amen.[55]

---

[55] Adapted from the Prayer of St. Francis of Assisi.

18. A Heart of Humility

BY CATH BUTLER

"The place God calls you to is the place where your deep gladness and the world's deep hunger meet."
—*Frederick Buechner*[56]

Read: Philippians 2:5-11

Hopefully, if you're reading this, you would at least consider calling yourself an artist... but what about a leader? So often we attach the idea of leadership to role and position, platform and charisma. But there is one popular definition of leadership that we all meet: "Leadership is influence."[57] Even if you don't have influence over

[56] Frederick Buechner, *Wishful Thinking: A Seekers ABC*, 1973, Harper & Row, pp.118-119
[57] John C. Maxwell, Developing the Leader Within You, 2012, Thomas Nelson, p.1

anyone else, you can certainly influence yourself—your own thoughts, attitudes, and actions. Like it or not, most of us also have influence (whether through action or inaction, speaking or silence) amongst friends, family, colleagues, and perhaps even more widely in our churches, communities, and organisations.

Whichever of those spheres applies to you, you are a leader—and your art is part of that. As artists, we lead both ourselves and others through the vehicle of our creativity. Many of us surely (if secretly) hope for the "success" of a significant sphere of influence in our making. I think that is hard wired into us—a desire to share what we have made, just like our Creator longed to share His creation with us. It can be a healthy pull that gives flow to our creating and stops it stagnating. But perhaps sometimes we forget that with influence comes leadership, and with leadership comes not just regard, but responsibility.

Let's look at another simple definition of leadership: service. The media may not emphasise this, but Jesus embodies it.[58] He changes our leadership lens, helping us to see how we're to have influence: not selfishly or vainly, but with humility and for the benefit of others.[59] It didn't matter to Him that His ministry was small and unknown (when He rode into Jerusalem on a donkey, people had to ask who He was[60]); His way was simply one of loving, generous response to the Father, expressed in self-giving, self-forgetful service.

Following in His footsteps is not easy. As an artist of congregational song and devotional writing, I know the pain of having to replace a beautifully poetic line with one of clearer

---

[58] Philippians 2:5-11

[59] Philippians 2:1-4

[60] Matthew 21:10

meaning, of taking out that crunchy chord with all its buzz to make the song more playable, or even of acknowledging that a song I was excited about in my living room just isn't landing with my small group and so won't reach a Sunday morning. There's a cost to this way of leading.

At the same time, Jesus didn't always put the cookies on the bottom shelf! His parables left people puzzled, He disappointed crowds by disappearing to pray and moving on to other villages, and He surprised and stretched His disciples' faith and understanding. Service doesn't mean spoon-feeding. It means knowing God's heart and those we serve so that we can offer creativity that speaks into their context in an appropriate and timely way. It means using our Spirit-sanctified artistry and awareness to decide when to remove roadblocks and when to offer an obstacle course. Above all, it means living like Jesus by laying ourselves down—laying our art down—out of obedience, even if it feels like death, so that one day every knee might bow at His name.[61]

As well as this Trinity-informed consciousness of the contexts and communities we serve, we also need a healthy dose of divinely illuminated self-awareness. We need to know ourselves to navigate the motives that move us, the calling upon us, the strengths and weaknesses that show up in our practice, and even the stage of artistic maturity evident in our craft. When we're at playschool, we confidently expect everything we make to be displayed prominently. As we move through our education, we begin to realise that quality is a spectrum, and that whilst some of what we create is "performance," much is "practice." By the time we enter the workplace, we have a more developed appreciation both of what it takes to produce

---

[61] Philippians 2:10-11

something fit for purpose, and of the suitability of the work we offer. What if we, as God's artists, were known for our creative maturity, our ability to discern when our pieces are ready, and what sphere our work is for? What if we were known for prioritising the people we serve over the product of our artistry?

Without this heart of humility, we can end up disappointed at best and damaging at worst. With it, we can cultivate a creativity that is a loving response to being beloved of God, that brings Him great glory and us deep gladness as it serves and satisfies the deep hunger around us.

APPLICATION

Imagine one of your pieces of art personified as a leader—draw or paint it, even. What would you desire for and expect of it as such? Ask some questions of it: who, where, or what is this artwork leading people to? How is it leading and serving them? Why is it leading them there (why do they need its leadership)? When might it serve and lead them best?

PRAYER

Father, thank You so much for the opportunities You give me to lead and influence myself and others with my art. I feel the weight of that responsibility and ask You to help me carry it lightly and joyfully by learning Your ways in it. Let me serve You and others out of deep love, and give me Your awareness and perspective as I offer my creativity to that end.

19. In Unwanted Places

by Peter Assad

"When the Lord saw that Leah was hated, He opened her womb."
—Genesis 29:31 (KJV)

I was 16 when I wrote my first song. Since then, I've come to find that being an artist means lots of practice dealing with rejection. Whether for radio stations, playlists, or album submissions, it remains a constant companion.

So I decided one day to take a tally. Scouring texts, emails, and social media, I counted all the times I received a direct "no" or was ghosted after follow-ups. In less than two years, my art was rejected 768 times. That's not even the total number—just when I stopped counting.

There's something deeply painful about hearing that you're unwanted 768 times.

Whether in our relationships, careers, or craft, it's nearly impossible to evade the sting of rejection. It reminds me of a story we often tell from the perspective of a man named Jacob—this time, through the lens of another character. Her name is Leah.

Overshadowed by her more beautiful sister, Leah was overlooked. In a cruel twist, her father tricked Jacob into marrying them both, leaving Leah to share a husband. Adding insult to injury, her father's scheme seemed to declare that no one would ever truly love her.

But then, in Genesis 29:31, we read this powerful truth: "When the Lord saw that Leah was hated, He opened her womb." God chose the unwanted, blessing her with children.

God also worked through the unwanted. One of Leah's sons became part of the family line of King David—and through that line, our Redeemer, Jesus Christ, entered human history. God literally used Leah's rejection to bring salvation to the whole world!

And then think about Jesus. Rejected by His own people, mocked, beaten, and crucified, Jesus became the ultimate unwanted. Why? To show that He loves the unwanted. And now, as His people, He calls us to love the unwanted too.

Imagine it for a second: a place where all the unwanted... are wanted!

- ❖ Where the homeless find a home.
- ❖ Where the foreigner finds refuge.
- ❖ Where the disabled are celebrated for who they are, not judged for what they're not.
- ❖ Where the elderly are honored, and their wisdom is cherished.
- ❖ Where the single and celibate are embraced, not seen as less-than.

❖ Where children aren't a nuisance but welcomed, just as Jesus said, "Let the little children come to me."[62]

This is what God envisions for His family, the Church: a community where the rejected are embraced, the unwanted are welcomed, and all are valued. Who better for God to choose than artists—who know the sting of rejection so deeply—to help build this kind of community, where the lost are found, the abandoned are loved, and the unwanted are wanted?

But maybe rejection has left you bitter. I get it, really. And so does Leah. In fact, for all the good she came to see, she still had major lapses where she was eaten up inside by it all. The truth of this Scripture comes to mind: "When they hurled their insults at Him, He did not retaliate... Instead, He entrusted Himself to [God] who judges justly" (1 Pe. 2:23).

You have the eternal eyes of the One who matters most in the universe—even when others don't see you, God does. And He wants you. Lord, help my heart believe.

APPLICATION

When you feel rejected—whether relationally, professionally, or in any other area of life—remember: God specializes in working through the rejected. Your rejection doesn't disqualify you; if anything, it may actually position you for God to do something powerful through you. The next time you're rejected, ask yourself: how can I lean into this season? How might God be preparing me to help the unwanted around me find their place in His love?

---

[62] Matthew 19:14

Lord, thank You for choosing Leah and thank You for choosing me. Our worth is not defined by the world's standards, but by Your unfailing love. When I feel overlooked, help me remember that You see me, You choose me, and You can work through every situation. Help me embrace my identity in You and empower me to love others as You have loved me.

20. Multiplying Light

BY AIMEE SMITH

"In the same way, let your light shine before others, that they may see your good deeds and glorify your Father in heaven."
— Matthew 5:16

The light that shone before me—when I was a shy, four-year-old little girl—was from Miss Delila (even though she was married, every woman in the South is a "Miss"). She was our church organist and pianist, and soon became my piano teacher. I remember being mesmerized by her beauty, her laughter, and the emotional, intricate way she played. She'd invite me to sit next to her on the organ bench during services, surrounded by soaring melodies, as my little kindergarten legs dangled, and her heels and toes danced across the pedals. In this way, good art draws others in: more than mere spectators, we become participants—caught up in the beauty and wonder of what has been created.

For the next fourteen years, I visited her home weekly for lessons—learning not just scales and technique, but life lessons and biblical truths too. She loved Jesus, served faithfully as a church musician, and taught hundreds of students—perhaps over a thousand —in the course of her career. She never hid her talent but poured it out for God's glory.

I often wonder who and what shaped her as an artist. Who sat at her elbow, guiding her hands? What music, moments, and people planted the seeds that became the woman I knew? Art rarely springs from nothing—it grows from the songs we sing as children, the beauty of nature, the discipline of craft, the example of others. Not every influence needs to be a formal teacher—sometimes it's a peer whose work inspires you, a book that ignites something, or the quiet pull of a sunset that compels you to create.

Miss Delila was one of those profound influences for me. She was "good soil... who produces a crop, yielding a hundred, sixty or thirty times what was sown."[63] The fruit of her labor has multiplied through the work of the Holy Spirit in me, and I'm just one of many students shaped by her faithful service.

More than a pianist, she inspired me to follow Jesus wherever He leads. That path eventually took me to Asia as a missionary, where I now teach music to more than 400 elementary students each week —most of whom don't know Jesus. Sometimes I wonder who they will sit beside one day, and in what different ways the light they've glimpsed might continue to shine long after I'm gone.

For years, I treated my musical gifts like a hobby, even as I served in music ministry. It wasn't until later that I surrendered them fully to the Lord, realizing our gifts are entrusted to us "to serve

---

[63] Matthew 13:23

others, as faithful stewards of God's grace."[64] I trust His call and leave the results in His hands, continually encouraged that "He who began a good work in [me] will carry it on to completion."[65]

A few years ago, Miss Delila passed away from cancer. She taught and served for as long as she could. Her last message to me—after hearing I was scheduled to lead worship—was: "Praying for you as you lead others to the throne of our Lord!"

Now she is at that throne. I imagine her on an organ bench, and the One sitting next to her is Jesus. She is not watching Him play magnificently, but He is watching her play with joy—throwing her head back in laughter as she continues to glorify her precious Savior in the heavenly realms.

APPLICATION

Prayerfully consider the following questions as you reflect on how the Holy Spirit is stirring your heart.

- ❖ Who has influenced you most in your creativity? How did their example shape you?
- ❖ Take a moment to thank them—perhaps through a letter, a visit, or by considering how to carry their influence forward in your own work.
- ❖ In what ways are you following Jesus and letting Him shape your craft, rather than following the craft alone?
- ❖ How have you seen your own creativity inspire, encourage, or guide someone else toward Jesus?

---

[64] 1 Peter 4:10
[65] Philippians 1:6

PRAYER

Lord, we come to You and confess our shortcomings. We desire to embrace the gifts You have graciously given us, and work humbly to develop and hone our craft for Your glory. Forgive us for neglecting our gifts at times, or using them with some control or reservations. We surrender all to You, and know that You will help us to bear fruit as we shine Your light to others.

Reflective & Artistic Practices

BY CATH BUTLER

"The best and most beautiful things in the world cannot be seen or even touched—
they must be felt with the heart."
—Helen Keller[66]

PART 1: VISIO DIVINA

For this *Visio Divina*, you will need to gather objects that symbolise how God has been speaking to you through this section—Walking with the Kingdom. You might want to choose one object per chapter or just pick one or two that represent how God has been speaking to you overall. Talk to God as you search these out, asking Him to open your eyes to significant symbols and your heart to what has been meaningful this week.

Once you have gathered your symbols, spend a few moments settling as you bring yourself into God's loving gaze.

Take each object one at a time and engage your senses to notice it fully:

66 Helen Keller, *The Story of My Life*, 1903, Doubleday, Page & Co., p.203

- ❖ What details are your eyes drawn to?
- ❖ What sounds is it capable of making?
- ❖ How does it feel under your fingers?
- ❖ Where does the smell of it take you?
- ❖ When you taste it, how do you react?

Now, allow your heart to ponder how these observations speak into what God has been doing with you as we have walked with the Kingdom this week. You might want to journal your thoughts and feelings.

Finally, offer these symbols and your reflections back to God, asking Him to bring to completion the good work He has begun in you.

PART 2: ARTISTIC PRACTICE

For this artistic practice, you are encouraged to choose a medium different to your primary mode of creative expression. If you're a song writer, go find some clay; if you're a dancer, pick up a pen; if you're a painter, why not try textiles of some sort?

The brief is simple: imagine yourself walking with the Kingdom, living from what God has been working in you this week, and what the future would look like because of that—both within and around you. Then create something that expresses what the Spirit-sanctified eyes of your imagination see. Have fun with this—allow yourself to lean into the freedom, possibility, and exuberance of it!

Pray this prayer to begin and close your practice:

King Jesus, I'm so grateful that I get to walk with Your Kingdom. Help my heart to see all the ways that You have already begun bringing it in me, around me, and even through me. Show me how I can partner with You as You continue building it and welcoming us into it. Amen.

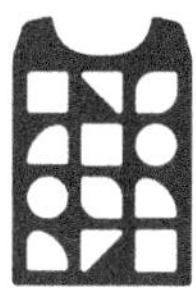

PART FIVE:
WALKING FORWARD

"There is in us an instinct for newness, for renewal, for a liberation of creative power. We seek to awaken in ourselves a force which really changes our lives from within. And yet the same instinct tells us that this change is a recovery of that which is deepest, most original, most personal in ourselves. To be born again is not to become somebody else, but to become ourselves."
—Thomas Merton[67]

---

67 Thomas Merton, *Choosing to Love the World: On Contemplation*, 2008, Sounds True, p.29

21. Make That Art

BY PETER ASSAD

> *"There is a crack, a crack in everything*
> *That's how the light gets in."*
> —*Leonard Cohen*[68]

You have walked the path. You have wrestled and wondered, listened and longed. You have prayed through resistance, gathered courage in the quiet, and leaned into the truth that your art matters—because you matter, and God calls you His own.

Now is the time—to move from reflection to response, to leave the shores of preparation and wade into waters deep. Not because you are fearless, but because the One who calls you is faithful.

You may never feel like you're ready enough, brave enough, or genius enough. Yet you are chosen—formed in the image of the

---

68 Leonard Cohen, *Anthem,* The Future, 1992, Columbia Records

Creator God. Your hands were made for making, your voice for speaking, and your vision for seeing what others cannot and even will not. You were made to be a witness.

Make that art.

Not to impress, but to invite; not to prove, but to praise; not to earn, but to offer art that tells the truth, splits the silence, and lets a little light in. Make art that brings justice and beauty to what's otherwise cracked and broken—art that sings of hope in the mourning and dares to believe for resurrection in the valley of death's shadow.

There will be times when the canvas stays blank, when your hands forget what they know, when the work feels too small or too slow. On those days, remember: the Spirit still hovers over the formless and void, for His mercies are new every morning.

This is your commissioning, for the One who shaped galaxies and desert flowers has also shaped you—with great intricacy and intentionality. You are no mistake, and neither is your art and artistry. Your desire to create is not a distraction from the Christian life, but a vital expression of it!

Resist the voices that say it's not holy enough, useful enough, or practical enough. Resist the lie that creativity is a luxury. Beauty is not excess, but essential. The Kingdom comes in like poetry—unexpected, subversive, and true.

You are part of that unfolding.

So take up your brush, your camera, your words. Pick up your instrument, your yarn, your pens. Whether you are stitching fabric or forming clay, composing harmonies or choreographing movement—make what only you can make.

There is someone awaiting the sound of our song and the vulnerability of our verse. We don't need to go viral, but when we offer our meager loaves and fish, God is still faithful to do the multiplying.

We may never know the impact our art will have—that's okay. Outcomes belong to the Lord, but obedience is our part. What matters isn't how many have seen it, but that we've seen it through.

Beauty is the seed of the world to come. Your work, when done in love, is never wasted. It is gathered. It is known. Make it afraid, if you must—but make it. Make it when no one's looking. Make it when you don't know what comes next. Make it when you're filled with doubt. Make it when joy overflows.

Let this be your benediction:

In the name of the Father,
  who formed you from the dust and called you good—make that art.
In the name of the Son,
  who came to redeem a world awaiting restoration—make that art.
In the name of the Spirit,
  who broods over chaos and births new things—make that art.

APPLICATION

What are you waiting for...? Make that art!

PRAYER

As You have been, be with me still. In the making, in the breaking, in the turmoil of brooding and the triumph of flow, may I find You ever before me—Father, Son, Spirit. Amen.

Concluding Reflective Practice

by Cath Butler

"The journey, not the arrival, matters."
—attr. T.S. Eliot

What a journey we have been on these past few weeks, walking with the Creator, with our calling, with our craft, and with the Kingdom. This final reflective practice is an opportunity to review the path God has led you by, remembering its beauty, recognising how it has formed you, and realising the signposts it offers you for the way ahead.

As you begin, use a simple breath prayer (like "You are here; I am with You," or "Abba Father, I am Yours") to bring yourself before God.

Take some time to review the road this devotional has accompanied you on. You might want to read back through your journal, sit with any art you have made, or simply allow a "highlights reel" to play in your mind's eye.

Then, on a new page in your journal or a fresh sheet of paper, draw a map of the path you have travelled. You could depict the terrain (mountains, valleys, rivers, forests, cliffs), landmarks, places of habitation, people, gifts, and invitations you've received along the way... whatever helps you to capture the journey of these past weeks. Feel free to annotate the map and its features too, using labels to add character and expression ("the rapids of rejection," "the woods of wonder," "the castle of calling," "the lamplight of legacy").

Once you have drawn your map, add some blank, forward-pointing signposts at the end of the path. On each signpost, name a direction God is asking you to pursue as you continue your creative journey with Him.

Lastly, allow your map to prompt prayerful conversation with God—gratitude, questions, realisations, resolve, dreams, declarations of hope—whatever bubbles up in your spirit as you pause in this place of looking back and looking forward, with Him at your side.

CONTRIBUTOR BIOGRAPHIES

Grace Assad (Missouri, US):
Grace is a follower of Jesus, an image-bearer, wife and mother, NICU nurse, educator, and storyteller at heart. She seeks to weave threads of God's beauty and truth through every part of her life—whether walking alongside her kids, guiding others in Scripture, writing songs that give voice to raw human experience, or holding space for families in the sacred vulnerability of the NICU. Above all, she longs to create spaces where people feel seen, valued, and invited to encounter the heart of Christ.

Peter Assad (Missouri, US):
The son of two Middle Eastern immigrants, Peter is an artist, catalyst, communicator, father, husband, pastor, and songwriter. Shaped by a rich cultural heritage and a deep well of personal experience, his work blends raw honesty with spiritual depth, creating spaces where others can bring their whole selves—all their questions, wounds, and wonder—into the Presence of God. He is the developer of Creative Compass, a tool for self-discovery and team building, designed to help others step more fully into their God-given callings. For more, visit poemsofgrace.com.

Rebecca Beese (England, UK):
Rebecca Beese is a worship leader and songwriter based in West Oxfordshire, UK. As a part of the United Adoration UK Team, she works in the Oxfordshire and Home Counties areas of England. She has a passion to nurture authentic Spirit-led worship in the churches she serves, facilitating them singing songs and creating artworks that

tell their own stories. Rebecca divides her time between being a wife and mum, teaching music, songwriting, leading worship, and training and developing others. Her heart is to see God's people released into all that He has for them. For more, visit www.rebeccabeese.co.uk.

Cath Butler (Northern Ireland, UK):
Cath enjoys working as a peripatetic music tutor, nurturing her own and others' creativity, leading worship, and offering spiritual direction. She is a member of the United Adoration UK Team, writes for Scripture Union's *Daily Bread*, and finds endless joy in the adventure of song writing. Her primary "love languages" are the clarinet, pancakes, reading, and journaling. Based in the beautiful coastal city of Bangor, you will often find her walking by the waves.

John Elkins (Texas, USA):
J. Novis Elkins is a pastor, author, artist, and speaker in South Texas. Alongside his wife, Stephanie, and their four children, Elkins strives to cultivate God's beauty in every aspect of life. The Elkins believe that it is the responsibility of every Christian to make their world a more beautiful place by living a life consistent with the gospel of Jesus Christ. They live a deeply simple life, delighting in the beauty of knowing Jesus and loving their community of faith. To learn more about the work and ministry of J. Novis Elkins, please visit www.jnoviselkins.com.

Dave Frincke (Indiana, USA):
Dave is an artist, Anglican priest, and president of United Adoration, a global movement dedicated to seeing the Church be the model of beauty, creativity, and artistry on the earth. He travels extensively, partnering with churches around the world to develop local, gospel-

centered creative communities. He lives in Fort Wayne, Indiana on the "Frincke Farm" with his wife and four kids.

Sharon Jones (Northern Ireland, UK):
Sharon lives and writes in rural County Antrim, Northern Ireland. She teaches literary studies and education at Stranmillis University College Belfast, and is an inaugural Fellow of The Inklings Project, University of Notre Dame. Sharon serves in music ministry in her local church and is a member of New Irish Arts. Married for almost thirty years to Mark, she is Mom to three young adults and an emerging survivor of the empty nest. A summer girl at heart, Sharon loves traveling, gardens, and the sea.

Kathryn Kircher (Indiana, USA):
Kathryn Kircher is the author of *Parables of the Eucalyptus: An Experiential Stay-at-Home Retreat* and a contributor to *A Place of Beauty, Not Coincidentally,* and *Your Breath, Our Tears*. When she's not busy facilitating United Adoration events with her husband, Nick, or scribbling away at her next story, you'll probably find Kathryn trying to spot an elusive warbler in the backyard, testing an international recipe in the kitchen, or being gleefully outsmarted by her grandkids in a board game. Find her online at kathrynmkircher.com.

Hunter Lynch (Mississippi, USA):
Hunter is the Worship and Youth Pastor at Highland Baptist Church in Vicksburg, MS. He and his wife, Ellie, have two daughters, Laney and Emmy, who are both avid songwriters. He has been writing for the Church since college and has served as an Online Songshare Leader for United Adoration for the past three years. His passion is for the local church to be equipped by songs that are melodically

accessible and lyrically substantial, and his joy is writing those songs with good company. He has served at Highland Baptist for seven years and looks forward to many more, Lord willing!

Elise Massa (England, UK):
Elise serves as the United Adoration UK Team Leader and as a worship music leader at her local church. Her music can be found on various streaming platforms, and she occasionally writes songs with Resound Worship and Jubilate Hymns. In her spare time, she can be found cheering her son on at football, drinking Yorkshire tea, taking pictures of flowers, and looking for the ever elusive hedgehog. She and her family currently live in Durham, England.

Cameron Miller (Indiana, USA):
Cameron is a writer, game designer, armchair economist, and amateur theologian. He is developing an online game called *Archons*, which seeks to create a common world for roleplaying and cooperative storytelling. He maintains a blog of his writings at www.puppycatproductions.com.

Catherine & Henry Miller (Florida, USA):
The first time Henry and Catherine wrote a song together in 2007, they each knew they had found a life-long partner. Three kids, two cats, a dog, and 17 years later, they enjoy working together, editing, and songwriting as a couple. Catherine is a singer-songwriter, writer, and pianist, and holds a BME from Florida State University and a Masters in Worship Studies from The Robert E. Webber Institute for Worship Studies in Jacksonville, FL. Henry is a poet and writer, with an interest in Wendell Berry and family agri-ventures. Based in

Tallahassee, FL, they enjoy Nerf battles, playing with their three rambunctious boys, and traveling.

Jimmy Orr (England, UK):
Jimmy Orr is a creative "jack-of-all-trades"—artist, poet, singer-songwriter, and author of *Don't Just Do Something, Stand There*—who is passionate about expressing faith and the human experience with honesty and imagination. Based in the UK, he serves on the United Adoration UK Team, leads UA retreats, curates worship, and lives a creative life with his family.

Nancy (Nethercott) Rund (Indiana & Texas, USA):
Nancy names her art forms as liturgical arts (all things planning and leading times of worship and retreat), and culinary arts (all things related to creating lovely, healthy, foods from around the world to serve to friends and family). She served 30 years as a missionary in Japan and now makes Indianapolis, IN, and Austin, TX, her home bases while continuing to minister internationally. Nancy serves on United Adoration's Board and on the Executive Team as Lead Chaplain.

Aimee Smith (Bangkok, Thailand):
Aimee Smith is a missionary, musician, wife, and mom. She is currently the United Adoration Thailand Team Leader, and is enjoying creative arts ministries on the mission field. In addition to teaching music, she enjoys leading worship and writing music. She has recently begun studying the theology of worship in seminary, and is looking forward to a season of encouraging other artists in worship.

Michael Stalcup (Bangkok, Thailand):
Michael is a Thai American poet living in Bangkok, Thailand, where he serves as a leader for United Adoration. His poems have been published in *Commonweal, First Things, The Lent Project, Rabbit Room Poetry, Sojourners*, and elsewhere. Michael co-leads Spirit & Scribe, a workshop helping writers integrate spiritual formation and writing craft, and the PAX Fellowship's Writing Cohort. You can find all of his poetry and teaching at michaelstalcup.com.

ACKNOWLEDGEMENTS

United Adoration is a movement of pastors and artists who want to see creativity revitalized in the local church.

To God our Father, the Son, and the Holy Spirit: thank You for creating us, saving us, and inspiring our work.

To Peter Assad and Cath Butler, who poured their energy into pulling together this collection;

To Cameron Miller, who worked diligently on content for UA's online blog that inspired this devotional, and all those who contributed to *A Place of Beauty*, the previous UA devotional that also shaped this one;

To Dave Frincke, who always encourages us to listen to God and creates space for us to try new things;

To all of our intercessors around the world, who cover us in prayer;

To the families and friends of each contributor, who read drafts, encouraged, and supported in manifold ways;

To all who donated to United Adoration and made this publication possible;

To all the local churches, pastors, and artists around the world: Thank you. Your work is beautiful.

Cover Art: Peter Assad

Editors: Cath Butler & Peter Assad

Formatting & Print Preparation: Dave Frincke

www.ingramcontent.com/pod-product-compliance
Lightning Source LLC
Chambersburg PA
CBHW051809050726
47598CB00006B/2488